Alonzo Trévier Jones

Civil Government and Religion

Or Christianity and the American Constitution

Alonzo Trévier Jones

Civil Government and Religion
Or Christianity and the American Constitution

ISBN/EAN: 9783337027605

Printed in Europe, USA, Canada, Australia, Japan

Cover: Foto ©Lupo / pixelio.de

More available books at **www.hansebooks.com**

CIVIL GOVERNMENT

AND

RELIGION,

OR

CHRISTIANITY AND THE AMERICAN CONSTITUTION.

By ALONZO T. JONES.

AMERICAN SENTINEL,
1059 CASTRO ST., OAKLAND, CAL.; 43 BOND ST., NEW YORK.;
26 AND 28 COLLEGE PLACE, CHICAGO, ILL.
1889.

PREFACE.

THIS little work is the outgrowth of several lectures upon the relationship between religion and the civil power, delivered in Minneapolis, Minn., in October, 1888. The interest manifested in the subject, and numerous requests for the publication of the main points of the arguments presented, have led to the issuing of this pamphlet. It is not intended to be exhaustive in its discussion of any point upon which it treats, but only suggestive in all. The subject is always interesting and important, and as there is now a persistent demand being made for religious legislation, especially in relation to Sunday-keeping, this subject has become worthy of more careful study than it has ever received in this country since the adoption of the national Constitution. The quotations and references presented, with connecting arguments, are designed simply to furnish the reader a ready reference, and directions to further study of the subject. It is hoped that the facts presented will awaken more interest in the study of the Constitution of the United States, and may lead to a better understanding of men's rights and liberties under it, than is commonly shown; and also to a closer study of the relation that should exist between civil government and religion, according to the words of Christ and the American Constitution.   A. T. J.

Feb. 13, 1889.

CONTENTS.

(4)

CIVIL GOVERNMENT AND RELIGION.

CHAPTER I.

CHRISTIANITY AND THE ROMAN EMPIRE.

JESUS CHRIST came into the world to set men free, and to plant in their souls the genuine principle of liberty, — liberty actuated by love, — liberty too honorable to allow itself to be used as an occasion to the flesh, or for a cloak of maliciousness, — liberty led by a conscience enlightened by the Spirit of God, — liberty in which man may be free from all men, yet made so gentle by love that he would willingly become the servant of all, in order to bring them to the enjoyment of this same liberty. This is freedom indeed. This is the freedom which Christ gave to man ; for whom the Son makes free, is free indeed. In giving to men this freedom, such an infinite gift could have no other result than that which Christ intended ; namely, to bind them in everlasting, unquestioning, unswerving allegiance to him as the royal benefactor of the race. He thus reveals himself to men as the highest good, and brings them to himself as the manifestation of that highest good, and to obedience to his will as the perfection of conduct. Jesus Christ was God manifest in the flesh. Thus God was in Christ reconciling the world to himself, that they might know him, the only true God, and Jesus Christ whom he sent. He gathered to himself disciples, instructed them in his heavenly doctrine, endued them with power from on high, sent them forth into all the world to preach this gospel of freedom to every creature, and to teach them

to observe all things whatsoever he had commanded
them.

The Roman empire then filled the world,— "the sub-
limest incarnation of power, and a monument the might-
iest of greatness built by human hands, which has upon
this planet been suffered to appear." That empire, proud
of its conquests, and exceedingly jealous of its claims, asserted its right to rule in all things, human and divine. As
in those times all gods were viewed as national gods, and
as Rome had conquered all nations, it was demonstrated
by this to the Romans that their gods were superior to all
others. And although Rome allowed conquered nations
to maintain the worship of their national gods, these, as
well as the conquered people, were yet considered only as
servants of the Roman States. Every religion, therefore,
was held subordinate to the religion of Rome, and though
"all forms of religion might come to Rome and take their
places in its Pantheon, they must come as the servants of
the State." The Roman religion itself was but the servant
of the State ; and of all the gods of Rome there were none
so great as the genius of Rome itself. The chief distinction of the Roman gods was that they belonged to the Roman State. Instead of the State deriving any honor from
the Roman gods, the gods derived their principle dignity
from the fact that they were the gods of Rome. This being so with Rome's own gods, it was counted by Rome
an act of exceeding condescension to recognize legally any
foreign god, or the right of any Roman subject to worship
any other gods than those of Rome. Neander quotes
Cicero as laying down a fundamental maxim of legislation
as follows : —

"No man shall have for himself particular gods of his
own ; no man shall worship by himself any new or foreign
gods, unless they are recognized by the public laws."—
Neander's Church History, vol. 1, pp. 86, 87. Torrey's
translation, Boston, 1852.

Thus it is seen that in the Roman view, the State took precedence of everything. The State was the highest idea of good. As expressed by Neander : —

"The idea of the State was the highest idea of ethics ; and within that was included all actual realization of the highest good ; hence the development of all other goods pertaining to humanity, was made dependent on this."— Id. p. 86.

Man with all that he had was subordinated to the State ; he must have no higher aim ; he must seek no higher good. Thus every Roman citizen was a subject, and every Roman subject was a slave. Says Mommsen : —

"The more distinguished a Roman became, the less was he a free man. The omnipotence of the law, the despotism of the rule, drove him into a narrow circle of thought and action, and his credit and influence depended on the sad austerity of his life. The whole duty of man, with the humblest and greatest of the Romans, was to keep his house in order, and be the obedient servant of the State."

It will be seen at once that for any man to profess the principles and the name of Christ, was virtually to set himself against the Roman empire ; for him to recognize God as revealed in Jesus Christ as the highest good, was but treason against the Roman State. It would not be looked upon by Rome as anything else than high treason, because the Roman State representing to the Roman the highest idea of good, for any man to assert that there was a higher good, and thus make Rome itself subordinate, would not be looked upon in any other light by Roman pride than that such an assertion was a direct blow at the dignity of Rome, and subversive of the Roman State. Consequently the Christians were not only called "atheists," because they denied the gods, but the accusation against them before the tribunals was for the crime of "high treason," because they denied the right of the State to interfere with men's relations to God. The accusation was that they were "irreverent to the Cæsars, and enemies of the Cæsars and of the Roman people."

To the Christian, the word of God asserted with absolute authority: "Fear God, and keep his commandments; for this is the whole duty of man." Eccl. 12 : 13. To him, obedience to this word through faith in Christ, was eternal life This to him was the conduct which showed his allegiance to God as the highest good, — a good as much higher than that of the Roman State as the government of God is greater than was the government of Rome, as God is greater than man, as heaven is higher than earth, as eternity is more than time, and as eternal interests are of more value than temporal.

The Romans considered themselves not only the greatest of all nations and the one to whom belonged power over all, but they prided themselves upon being the most religious of all nations. Cicero commended the Romans as the most religious of all nations, because they carried their religion into all the details of life.

"The Roman ceremonial worship was very elaborate and minute, applying to every part of daily life. It consisted in sacrifices, prayers, festivals, and the investigations, by auguries and haruspices, of the will of the gods and the course of future events. The Romans accounted themselves an exceedingly religious people, because their religion was so intimately connected with the affairs of home and State. . . . Thus religion everywhere met the public life of the Roman by its festivals, and laid an equal yoke on his private life by its requisition of sacrifices, . prayers, and auguries. All pursuits must be conducted according to a system carefully laid down by the College of Pontiffs. . . . If a man went out to walk, there was a form to be recited; if he mounted his chariot, another." — *Ten Great Religions*, chap. 8.

The following extract from Gibbon will give a clear view of the all-pervading character of the Roman relig-

ious rites and ceremonies, and it also shows how absolutely the profession of the Christian religion made a
separation between the one who professed it and all
things pertaining to the affairs of Rome : —

"The religion of the nations was not merely a spec-
ulative doctrine professed in the schools or preached in
the temples. The innumerable deities and rites of Poly-
theism were closely interwoven with every circumstance
of business or pleasure, of public or of private life ; and
it seemed impossible to escape the observance of them,
without, at the same time, renouncing the commerce of
mankind and all the offices and amusements of society.
. . . The public spectacles were an essential part of the
cheerful devotion of the pagans, and the gods were supposed to accept, as the most grateful offering, the games
that the prince and people celebrated in honor of their
peculiar customs. The Christian, who with pious horror
avoided the abomination of the circus or the theater,
found himself encompassed with infernal snares in every
convivial entertainment, as often as his friends, invoking
the hospitable deities, poured out libations to each others'
happiness. When the bride, struggling with well-affected
reluctance, was forced in hymenial pomp over the thresh-
old of her new habitation, or when the sad procession of
the dead slowly moved toward the funeral pile, the Christian, on these interesting occasions, was compelled to
desert the persons who were dearest to him, rather than
contract the guilt inherent to those impious ceremonies.
Every art and every trade that was in the least concerned
in the framing or adorning of idols, was polluted by the
stain of idolatry.

"The dangerous temptations which on every side
lurked in ambush to surprise the unguarded believer,
assailed him with redoubled violence on the day of solemn festivals. So artfully were they framed and disposed
throughout the year, that superstition always wore the
appearance of pleasure, and often of virtue. . . . On the
days of general festivity, it was the custom of the an-
cients to adorn their doors with lamps and with branches
of laurel, and to crown their heads with garlands of flow-

ers. This innocent and elegant practice might have been tolerated as a mere civil institution. But it most un-luckily happened that the doors were under the protec-tion of the household gods, that the laurel was sacred to the lover of Daphne, and that garlands of flowers, though frequently worn as a symbol either of joy or mourning, had been dedicated in their first origin to the service of superstition. The trembling Christians who were per-suaded in this instance to comply with the fashions of their country and the commands of the magistrates, la-bored under the most gloomy apprehensions from the reproaches of their own conscience, the censures of the church, and the denunciations of divine vengeance."

All this clearly shows that to profess the name of Christ, a person was compelled to renounce every other relationship in life. He could not attend a wedding or a funeral of his nearest relatives, because every ceremony was performed with reference to the gods. He could not attend the public festival, for the same reason. More than this, he could not escape by not attending the pub-lic festival ; because on days of public festivity, the doors of the houses, and the lamps about them, and the heads of the dwellers therein, must all be adorned with laurel and garlands of flowers, in honor of the licentious gods and godesses of Rome. If the Christian took part in these services, he paid honor to the gods as did the other heathen. If he refused to do so, which he must do if he would obey God and honor Christ, he made himself con-spicuous before the eyes of all the people, all of whom were intensely jealous of the respect they thought due to the gods ; and also in so doing, the Christian disobeyed the Roman law, which commanded these things to be done. He thus became subject to persecution, and that meant death, because the law said : —

"Worship the gods in all respects according to the laws of your country, and compel all others to do the same. But hate and punish those who would introduce anything whatever alien to our customs in this particular."

And further : —

"Whoever introduces new religions, the tendency and character of which are unknown, whereby the minds of men may be disturbed, shall, if belonging to the higher rank, be banished ; if to the lower, punished with death."

This was the Roman law. Every Christian, merely by the profession of Christianity, severed himself from all the gods of Rome, and from everything that was done in their honor. And everything *was* done in their honor. The great mass of the first Christians were from the lower ranks of the people. The law said that if any of the lower ranks introduced new religions, they should be punished with death. The Christians, introducing a new religion, and being from the lower ranks, made themselves subject to death whenever they adopted the religion of Christ. This is why Paul and Peter, and multitudes of other Christians, suffered death for the name of Christ. Such was the Roman law, and when Rome put the Christians to death, it was not counted by Rome to be persecution. It would not for an instant be admitted that such was persecution. It was only enforcing the law. The State of Rome was supreme. The State ruled in religious things. Whoever presumed to disobey the law must suffer the penalty ; all that Rome did, all that it professed to do, was simply to enforce the law.

If the principle be admitted that the State has the right to legislate in regard to religion, and to enforce religious observances, then no blame can ever be attached to the Roman empire for putting the Christians to death. Nor can it be admitted that such dealings with the Christians was persecution. The enforcement of right laws can never be persecution, however severely the law may deal with the offender. To hang a murderer is not persecution. To hunt him down, even with blood-hounds, to bring him to, justice, is not persecution. We repeat, therefore, that the enforcement of right laws never can be persecution. If, therefore, religion or religious observances be a proper subject of legislation by civil government, then there never has been and there never can be any such thing as religious persecution. Because civil governments are ruled by majorities, the religion of the majority must of necessity be the adopted religion ; and if civil legislation in religious things be right, the majority may legislate in regard to their own religion. Such laws made in such a case must be right laws, and the enforcement of them therefore can never be persecution.

But all this, with the authority and all the claims of the Roman empire, is swept away by the principle of Christ, which every one then asserted who named the name of Christ, — that civil government can never of right have anything to do with religion or religious observances, — that religion is not a subject of legislation by any civil government, — that religion, religious profession, and religious observances must be left entirely between the individual and his God, to worship as his own conscience shall dictate, — that to God only is to be rendered that which is God's, while to Cæsar is to be rendered only that which is Cæsar's. This is the principle that Christ established, and which, by his disciples, he sent into all the world, and which they asserted wherever they went ; in behalf of which they forfeited every earthly consideration, endured untold torments, and for which they freely gave their lives. It was, moreover, because of the establishment of this principle by Jesus Christ, and the assertion of it by his true disciples, that we have to-day the rights and liberties which we enjoy. The following extract from Lecky is worthy to be recorded in letters of gold, and held in sorrowful, but ever grateful, remembrance : —

"Among the authentic records of pagan persecutions, there are histories which display, perhaps more vividly than any other, both the depth of cruelty to which human nature may sink, and the heroism of resistance it may attain. . . . The most horrible recorded instances of torture were usually inflicted, either by the populace, or in their presence in the arena. We read of Christians bound in chairs of red-hot iron, while the stench of their half-consumed flesh rose in a suffocating cloud to heaven ; of others who were torn to the very bone by shells or hooks of iron ; of holy virgins given over to the lusts of the gladiator, or to the mercies of the pander ; of two hundred and twenty-seven converts sent on one occasion to the mines, each with the sinews of one leg severed with a red-hot iron, and with an eye scooped from the socket ; of fires so slow that the victims writhed for hours in their agonies ; of bodies torn limb from limb, or sprinkled with burning lead ; of mingled salt and vinegar poured over the flesh that was bleeding from the rack ; of tortures prolonged and varied through entire days. For the love of their divine Master, for the cause they believed to be true, men, and even weak girls, endured these things without flinching, when one word would have freed them from their suffering. No opinion we may form of the proceedings of priests in a later age, should impair the reverence with which we bend before the martyr's tomb."—*History of European Morals*, end of chapter 3.

All this was endured by men and women and even weak girls, that people in future ages might be free. All this was endured in support of the principle, that with religion, civil government cannot of right have anything to do. All this was endured that men might be free, and that all future ages might know it to be the inalienable right of every soul to worship God according to the dictates of his own conscience.

CHAPTER II.

"THEN went the Pharisees, and took counsel how they might entangle him in his talk. And they sent out unto him their disciples with the Herodians, saying, Master, we know that thou art true, and teachest the way of God in truth ; neither carest thou for any man, for thou regardest not the person of men. Tell us therefore, What thinkest thou? Is it lawful to give tribute unto Cæsar, or not? But Jesus perceived their wickedness, and said, Why tempt ye me, ye hypocrites? Show me the tribute money. And they brought unto him a penny. And he saith unto them, Whose is this image and super- scription? They say unto him, Cæsar's. Then saith he unto them, Render therefore unto Cæsar the things which are Cæsar's, and unto God the things that are God's."

In these words Christ has established a clear distinc- tion between Cæsar and God, — between that which is Cæsar's and that which is God's ; that is, between the civil and the religious power, and between what we owe to the civil power and what we owe to the religious power. That which is Cæsar's is to be rendered to Cæsar ; that which is God's is to be rendered to God alone. With that which is God's, Cæsar can have noth- ing to do. To say that we are to render to Cæsar that which is God's, or that we are to render to God, by Cæsar, that which is God's, is to pervert the words of Christ,

(14)

and make them meaningless. Such an interpretation would be but to entangle him in his talk,—the very thing that the Pharisees sought to do.

As the word *Cæsar* refers to civil government, it is apparent at once that the duties which we owe to Cæsar are civil duties, while the duties which we owe to God are wholly moral or religious duties. Webster's definition of *religion* is,—

"The recognition of God as an object of worship, love, and obedience."

Another definition, equally good, is as follows : —

"Man's personal relation of faith and obedience to God."

It is evident, therefore, that religion and religious duties pertain solely to God ; and as that which is God's is to be rendered to him and not to Cæsar, it follows inevitably that according to the words of Christ, civil government can never of right have anything to do with religion,—with a man's personal relation of faith and obedience to God.

Another definition which may help in making the distinction appear, is that of *morality*, as follows : —

"*Morality:* The relation of conformity or non-conformity to the true moral standard or rule. . . . The conformity of an act to the divine law."

As morality, therefore, is the conformity of an act to the divine law, it is plain that morality also pertains solely to God, and with that, civil government can have nothing to do. This may appear at first sight to be an extreme position, if not a false one ; but it is not. It is the correct position, as we think any one can see who will give the subject a little careful thought. The first part of the definition already given, says that morality is "the relation of conformity or non-conformity to the true moral standard or rule," and the latter part of the definition shows that this true moral standard is the divine law. Again : Moral law is defined as —

"The will of God, as the supreme moral ruler, concerning the character and conduct of all responsible beings ; the rule of action as obligatory on the conscience or moral nature." "The moral law is summarily contained in the decalogue, written by the finger of God on two tables of stone, and delivered to Moses on Mount Sinai."

These definitions are evidently according to Scripture. The Scriptures show that the ten commandments are the law of God ; that they express the will of God ; that they pertain to the conscience, and take cognizance of the thoughts and intents of the heart ; and that obedience to these commandments is the duty that man owes to God.   Says the Scripture, —

"Fear God, and keep his commandments ; for this is the whole duty of man."   Eccl. 12 : 13.

And the Saviour says, —

"Ye have heard that it was said by them of old time, Thou shalt not kill ; and whosoever shall kill shall be in danger of the judgment ; but I say unto you that whosoever is angry with his brother without a cause, shall be in danger of the judgment ; and whosoever shall say to his brother, Raca [vain fellow, *margin*], shall be in danger of the council ; but whosoever shall say, Thou fool, shall be in danger of hell fire."   Matt. 5 : 21, 22.

The apostle John, referring to the same thing, says, —

"Whosoever hateth his brother is a murderer." 1 John 3 : 15.

Again, the Saviour says, —

"Ye have heard that it was said by them of old time, Thou shalt not commit adultery ; but I say unto you that whosoever looketh on a woman to lust after her, hath committed adultery with her already in his heart."   Matt. 5 : 27, 28.

Other illustrations might be given, but these are sufficient to show that obedience to the moral law is morality; that it pertains to the thoughts and the intents of the heart, and therefore, in the very nature of the case, lies beyond the reach or control of the civil power. To hate, is murder; to covet, is idolatry; to think impurely of a woman, is adultery;—these are all equally immoral, and violations of the moral law, but no civil government seeks to punish for them. A man may hate his neighbor all his life; he may covet everything on earth; he may think impurely of every woman that he sees,—he may keep it up all his days; but so long as these things are confined to his thought, the civil power cannot touch him. It would be difficult to conceive of a more immoral person than such a man would be; yet the State cannot punish him. It does not attempt to punish him. This demonstrates again that with morality or immorality the State can have nothing to do.

But let us carry this further. Only let that man's hatred lead him, either by word or sign, to attempt an injury to his neighbor, and the State will punish him: only let his covetousness lead him to lay hands on what is not his own, in an attempt to steal, and the State will punish him; only let his impure thought lead him to attempt violence to any woman, and the State will punish him. Yet bear in mind that even then the State does not punish him for his immorality, but for his incivility. The immorality lies in the heart, and can be measured by God only. The State punishes no man because he is immoral. If it did, it would have to punish as a murderer the man who hates another, because according to the true standard of morality, hatred is murder. Therefore it is clear that in fact the State punishes no man because he is immoral, but because he is uncivil. It cannot punish immorality; it must punish incivility.

2

This distinction is shown in the very term by which is designated State or national government ; it is called *civil* government. No person ever thinks of calling it moral government. The government of God is the only moral government. God is the only moral governor. The law of God is the only moral law. To God alone pertains the punishment of immorality, which is the transgression of the moral law. Governments of men are civil governments, not moral. Governors of men are civil governors, not moral. The laws of States and nations are civil laws, not moral. To the authorities of civil government pertains the punishment of incivility, that is, the transgression of civil law. It is not theirs to punish immorality. That pertains solely to the Author of the moral law and of the moral sense, who is the sole judge of man's moral relation. All this must be manifest to every one who will think fairly upon the subject, and it is confirmed by the definition of the word *civil*, which is as follows : —

"*Civil:* Pertaining to a city or State, or to a citizen in his relations to his fellow-citizens, or to the State."

By all these things it is made clear that we owe to Cæsar (civil government) only that which is civil, and that we owe to God that which is moral or religious. Other definitions show the same thing. For instance, sin as defined by Webster, is "any violation of God's will ; " and as defined by the Scriptures, "is the transgression of the law." That the law here referred to is the moral law — the ten commandments — is shown by Rom. 7 : 7 : —

"I had not known sin, but by the law ; for I had not known lust, except the law had said, Thou shalt not covet."

Thus the Scriptures show that sin is a transgression of the law which says, "Thou shalt not covet," and that is the moral law.

But crime is an offense against the laws of the State. The definition is as follows: —

"Crime is strictly a violation of law either human or divine; but in present usage the term is commonly applied to actions contrary to the laws of the State."

Thus civil statutes define crime, and deal with crime, but not with sin; while the divine statutes define sin, and deal with sin, but not with crime.

As God is the only moral governor, as his is the only moral government, as his law is the only moral law, and as it pertains to him alone to punish immorality, so likewise *the promotion of morality* pertains to him alone. Morality is conformity to the law of God; it is obedience to God. But obedience to God must spring from the heart in sincerity and truth. This it must do, or it is not obedience; for, as we have proved by the word of God, the law of God takes cognizance of the thoughts and intents of the heart. But "all have sinned, and come short of the glory of God." By transgression, all men have made themselves immoral. "Therefore by the deeds of the law [by obedience] there shall no flesh be justified [accounted righteous, or made moral] in his sight." Rom. 3 : 20. As all men have, by transgression of the law of God, made themselves immoral, therefore no man can, by obedience to the law, become moral; because it is that very law which declares him to be immoral. The demands, therefore, of the moral law, must be satisfied, before he can ever be accepted as moral by either the law or its Author. But the demands of the moral law can never be satisfied by an immoral person, and this is just what every person has made himself by transgression. Therefore it is certain that men can never become moral by the moral law.

From this it is equally certain that if ever men shall be made moral, it must be by the Author and Source of all morality. And this is just the provision which God has made. For, "now the righteousness [the morality] of God without the law is manifested, being witnessed by the law and the prophets; even the righteousness [the morality] of God which is *by faith of Jesus Christ* unto all and upon all them that believe; for there is no difference; for all have sinned [made themselves immoral], and come short of the glory of God." Rom. 3 : 21-23. It is by the morality of Christ alone that men can be made moral. And this morality of Christ is the morality of God, which is imputed to us for Christ's sake; and we receive it by faith in Him who is both the author and finisher of faith. Then by the Spirit of God the moral law is written anew in the heart and in the mind, sanctifying the soul unto obedience — unto morality. Thus, and thus alone, can men ever attain to morality; and that morality is the morality of God which is by faith of Jesus Christ; *and there is no other in this world.* Therefore, as morality springs from God, and is planted in the heart by the Spirit of God, through faith in the Son of God, it is demonstrated by proofs of Holy Writ itself, that *to God alone pertains the promotion of morality.*

God, then, being the sole promoter of morality, through what instrumentality does he work to promote morality in the world? What body has he made the conservator of morality in the world: the church, or the civil power; which? — The church, and the church alone. It is "the church of the living God." It is "the pillar and ground of the truth." It was to the church that he said, "Go ye into all the world, and preach the gospel to every creature;" "And, lo, I am with you alway, even unto the end of the world." It is by the church, through the preaching of Jesus Christ, that the gospel is "made known to all nations for the obedience of faith." There is no obedience but the obedience of faith; there is no morality but the morality of faith. Therefore it is proved that to the church, and *not* to the State, is committed the conservation of morality in the world. This at once settles the question as to whether the State shall teach **morality**, or religion.— The State *cannot* teach morality **or religion. It has not** the credentials **for it.** The Spirit **of God and the gospel of Christ are** both essential **to** the teaching **of morality, and neither of** these is committed **to the** State, but **both to the** church.

But though this work be committed to the **church,** even then there is not committed to **the church the pre-**rogative either to reward **morality or to punish** immoral-ity. She beseeches, **she entreats, she persuades men to** be reconciled to God ; **she trains them in the** principles and the **practice of morality. It is hers by moral** suasion or spiritual censures **to preserve the purity** and *discipline* of her membership. But hers it is **not** either to reward morality **or to punish immorality. This** pertains to God alone, because whether **it be** morality **or** immorality, it springs from the **secret** counsels of the heart ; and as God alone knows the heart, he **alone** can measure either the merit or the guilt involved in any question of morals.

By this it is demonstrated that to no man, **to** no assem-bly or organization of men, does there belong **any right** whatever **to** punish **immorality.** Whoever attempts it, usurps the prerogative **of God.** The Inquisition **is the** inevitable logic **of any claim of** any assembly **of men** to punish immorality, because to punish immorality, **it is** necessary in some way **to get at** the thoughts and intents of the heart. The **papacy,** asserting the **right** to compel men to **be moral, and to** punish **them for immorality,** had the **cruel** courage **to carry the evil principle** to its logical consequence. In carrying out the principle, it was found to be essential to **get at the** secrets of men's hearts ; **and** it was **found that the** diligent application of torture would wring from **men, in many** cases, a full confession of **the** most secret counsels of their hearts. Hence the Inquisition was established as the means best adapted to secure the desired end. So long as men grant the proposition that it is within the province of civil government to enforce morality, it is to very little purpose that they condemn the Inquisition ; for that tribunal is only the logical result of the proposition.

By all these evidences is established the plain, common-sense principle that to civil government pertains only that which the term itself implies, — that which is civil. The purpose of civil government is civil, and not moral. Its function is to preserve order in society, and to cause all its subjects to rest in assured safety, by guarding them against all incivility. Morality belongs to God ; civility, to the State. Morality must be rendered to God ; civility, to the State. "Render therefore unto Cæsar the things which are Cæsar's ; and unto God the things that are God's." *

But it may be asked, Does not the civil power enforce the observance of the commandments of God, which say, Thou shalt not steal, thou shalt not kill, thou shalt not commit adultery, and thou shalt not bear false witness? Does not the civil power punish the violation of these commandments of God ? *Answer.* — The civil power does not enforce these, nor does it punish the violation of them, *as commandments of God.* The State does forbid murder and theft and perjury, and some States forbid adultery, but not as commandments of God. From time immemorial, governments that knew nothing about God, have forbidden these things. If the civil power at-

---

* There is an accommodated sense in which the word *morality* is used, in which it is made to refer only to men's relations to their fellow-men ; and with reference to this view of morality, it is sometimes said that the civil power is to enforce morality *upon a civil basis.* But morality on a civil basis is only civility, and the enforcement of morality upon a civil basis is the enforcement of civility, and nothing else. Without the Inquisition it is impossible for civil government ever to carry its jurisdiction beyond civil things, or to enforce anything but civility.

tempted to enforce these as the commandments of God, it would have to punish as a murderer the man who hates another; it would have to punish as a perjurer the man who raises a false report; it would have to punish as an adulterer the person who thinks impurely; it would have to punish as a thief the man who wishes to cheat his neighbor; because all these things are violations of the commandments of God. Therefore if the State is to enforce these things as the commandments of God, it will have to punish the thoughts and intents of the heart; but this is not within the province of any earthly power, and it is clear that any earthly power that should attempt it, would thereby simply put itself in the place of God, and usurp his prerogative.

More than this, such an effort would be an attempt to punish sin, because transgression of the law of God is sin; but sins will be forgiven upon repentance, and God does not punish the sinner for the violation of his law, when his sins are forgiven. Now if the civil power undertakes to enforce the observance of the law of God, it cannot justly enforce that law upon the transgressor whom God has forgiven. For instance, suppose a man steals twenty dollars from his neighbor, and is arrested, prosecuted, and found guilty. But suppose that between the time that he is found guilty and the time when sentence is to be passed, the man repents, and is forgiven by the Lord. Now he is counted by the Lord as though he never had violated the law of God. The commandment of God does not stand against him for that transgression. And as it is the law of God that the civil law started out to enforce, the civil power also must forgive him, count him innocent, and let him go free. More than this, the statute of God says, "If thy brother trespass against thee, rebuke him; and if he repent, forgive him. And if he trespass against thee seven times in a day, and seven times in a day turn again to thee, saying, I repent; thou shalt forgive him." If civil government is to enforce the law of God, when a man steals, or commits perjury or any form of violence, and is arrested, if he says, " I repent," he must be forgiven; if he does it again, is again arrested, and again says, "I repent," he must be forgiven; and if he commits it seven times in a day, and seven times in a day says, "I repent," he must be forgiven. It will be seen at once that any such system would be utterly destructive of civil government; and this only demonstrates conclusively that no civil government can ever of right have anything to do with the enforcement of the commandments of God as such, or with making the Bible its code of laws.

God's government can be sustained by the forgiveness of the sinner to the uttermost, because by the sacrifice of Christ he has made provision "to save them to the uttermost that come unto God by him; seeing he ever liveth to make intercession for them;" but in civil government, if a man steals, or commits any other crime, and is apprehended and found guilty, it has nothing to do with the case if the Lord does forgive him; he must be punished.

The following remarks of Prof. W. T. Harris, late superintendent of public schools in the city of St. Louis, are worthy of careful consideration in this connection: —

"A crime, or breach of justice, is a deed of the individual, which the State, by its judicial acts, returns on the individual. The State furnishes a measure for crime, and punishes criminals according to their deserts. The judicial mind is a measuring mind, a retributive mind, because trained in the forms of justice which sees to it that every man's deed shall be returned to him, to bless him or to curse him with pain. Now, a sin is a breach of the law of holiness, a lapse out of the likeness to the divine form, and as such it utterly refuses to be measured. It is infinite death to lapse out of the form of the divine. A sin cannot be atoned for by any finite punishment, but only (as revelation teaches) by a divine act of sacrifice. . . . It would destroy the State to attempt to treat crimes as sins, and to forgive them in case of repentance. It would impose on the judiciary the business of going behind the overt act to the disposition or frame of mind within the depth of personality. But so long as the deed is not uttered in the act, it does not belong to society, but only to the individual and to God. No human institution can go behind the overt act, and attempt to deal absolutely with the substance of man's spiritual freedom. . . . Sin and crime must not be confounded, nor must the same deed be counted as crime and sin by the same authority. Look at it as crime, and it is capable of measured retribution. The law does not pursue the murderer beyond the gallows. He has expiated his crime with his life. But the slightest sin, even if it is no crime at all, as for example the anger of a man against his brother, an anger which does not utter itself in the form of violent deeds, but is pent up in the heart, — such noncriminal sin will banish the soul forever from heaven, unless it is made naught by sincere repentance."

The points already presented in this chapter are perhaps sufficient in this place to illustrate the principle announced in the word of Christ ; and although that principle is plain, and is readily accepted by the sober, common-sense thought of every man, yet through the selfish ambition of men the world has been long in learning and accepting the truth of the lesson. The United States is the first and only government in history that is based on the principle established by Christ. In Article VI. of the national Constitution, this nation says that "no religious test shall ever be required as a qualification to any office or public trust under the United States." By an amendment making more certain the adoption of the principle, it declares in the first amendment to the Constitution, "Congress shall make no law respecting an establishment of religion, or prohibiting the free exercise thereof." This first amendment was adopted in 1789, by the first Congress that ever met under the Constitution. In 1796 a treaty was made with Tripoli, in which it was declared (Article II.) that "the Government of the United States of America is not in any sense founded on the Christian religion." This treaty was framed by an ex-Congregationalist clergyman, and was signed by President Washington. It was not out of disrespect to religion or Christianity that these clauses were placed in the Constitution, and that this one was inserted in that treaty. On the contrary, it was entirely on account of their respect for religion, and the Christian religion in particular, as being beyond the province of civil government, pertaining solely to the conscience, and resting entirely between the individual and God. It was because of this that this nation was Constitutionally established according to the principle of Christ, demanding of men only that they render to Cæsar that which is Cæsar's, and leaving them entirely free to render to God that which is God's, if they choose, as they choose, and when they choose ; or, as expressed by Washington himself, in reply to an address upon the subject of religious legislation : —

"Every man who conducts himself as a good citizen, is accountable alone to God for his religious faith, and should be protected in worshiping God according to the dictates of his own conscience."

We cannot more fitly close this chapter than with the following tribute of George Bancroft to this principle, as embodied in the words of Christ, and in the American Constitution : —

"In the earliest States known to history, government and religion were one and indivisible. Each State had its special deity, and often these protectors, one after another, might be overthrown in battle, never to rise again. The Peloponnesian War grew out of a strife about an oracle. Rome, as it sometimes adopted into citizen-ship those whom it vanquished, introduced in like manner, and with good logic for that day, the worship of their gods. No one thought of vindicating religion for the conscience of the individual, till a voice in Judea, break-ing day for the greatest epoch in the life of humanity, by establishing a pure, spiritual, and universal religion for all mankind, enjoined to render to Cæsar only that which is Cæsar's. The rule was upheld during the infancy of the gospel for all men. No sooner was this religion adopted by the chief of the Roman empire, than it was shorn of its character of universality, and enthralled by an unholy connection with the unholy State ; and so it continued till the new nation, — the least defiled with the barren scoffings of the eighteenth century, the most gen-eral believer in Christianity of any people of that age, the chief heir of the Reformation in its purest forms, — when it came to establish a government for the United States, refused to treat faith as a matter to be regulated by a corporate body, or having a headship in a monarch or a State.

"Vindicating the right of individuality even in relig-ion, and in religion above all, the new nation dared to set the example of accepting in its relations to God the principle first divinely ordained of God in Judea. It left the management of temporal things to the temporal power ; but the American Constitution, in harmony with the people of the several States, withheld from the Federal Government the power to invade the home of reason, the citadel of conscience, the sanctuary of the soul ; and not from indifference, but that the infinite Spirit of eternal truth might move in its freedom and purity and power."— *History of the Formation of the Constitution*, last chapter.

Thus the Constitution of the United States as it is, stands as the sole monument of all history representing the principle which Christ established for earthly gov-ernment. And under it, in liberty, civil and religious, in enlightenment, and in progress, this nation has deserv-edly stood as the beacon-light of the world, for a hun-dred years.

CHAPTER III.

THE POWERS THAT BE.

IN support of the doctrine that civil government has the right to act in things pertaining to God, the text of Scripture is quoted which says, "The powers that be are ordained of God." This passage is found in Rom. 13 : 1. The first nine verses of the chapter are devoted to this subject, showing that the powers that be are ordained of God, and enjoining upon Christians, upon every soul in fact, the duty of respectful subjection to civil government. The whole passage reads as follows : —

"Let every soul be subject unto the higher powers. For there is no power but of God : the powers that be are ordained of God. Whosoever therefore resisteth the power, resisteth the ordinance of God ; and they that resist shall receive to themselves damnation. For rulers are not a terror to good works, but to the evil. Wilt thou then not be afraid of the power ? do that which is good, and thou shalt have praise of the same : for he is the minister of God to thee for good. But if thou do that which is evil, be afraid : for he beareth not the sword in vain ; for he is the minister of God, a revenger to execute wrath upon him that doeth evil. Wherefore ye must needs be subject not only for wrath, but also for conscience' sake. For, for this cause pay ye tribute also ; for they are God's ministers, attending continually upon this very thing. Render therefore to all their dues : tribute to whom tribute is due ; custom to whom custom ; fear to whom fear ; honor to whom honor. Owe no man anything, but to love one another ; for he that loveth another

hath fulfilled the law. For this, Thou shalt not commit
adultery, Thou shalt not kill, Thou shalt not steal, Thou
shalt not bear false witness, Thou shalt not covet: and
if there be any other commandment, it is briefly comprehended in this saying, namely, Thou shalt love thy neighbor as thyself."

It is easy to see that this scripture is but an exposition of the words of Christ, " Render to Cæsar the things
that are Cæsar's." In the Saviour's command to render
unto Cæsar the things that are Cæsar's, there is plainly a
recognition of the rightfulness of civil government, and
that civil government has claims upon us which we are
in duty bound to recognize, and that there are things
which duty requires us to render to the civil government.
This scripture in Romans 13 simply states the same thing
in other words: " Let every soul be subject unto the
higher powers. For there is no power but of God: the
powers that be are ordained of God."

Again, the Saviour's words were called out by a question concerning tribute. They said to him, " Is it lawful
to give tribute unto Cæsar, or not?" Rom. 13 : 6 refers
to the same thing, saying, " For, for this cause pay ye tribute also; for they are God's ministers, attending continually upon this very thing." In answer to the question of
the Pharisees about the tribute, Christ said, " Render
therefore unto Cæsar the things which are Cæsar's."
Rom. 13 : 7, taking up the same thought, says, " Render
therefore to all their dues: tribute to whom tribute is
due; custom to whom custom; fear to whom fear; honor
to whom honor." These references make positive that
which we have stated, — that this portion of Scripture
(Rom. 13 : 1–9) is a divine commentary upon the words of
Christ in Matt. 22 : 17–21.

In the previous chapter we have shown by many proofs
that civil government has nothing to do with anything
that pertains to God. If the argument in that chapter is

sound, then Rom. 13 : 1-9, being the Lord's commentary upon the words which are the basis of that argument, ought to confirm the position there taken. And this it does.

The passage in Romans refers first to civil government, the higher powers, — not the highest power, but the powers that be. Next it speaks of rulers, as bearing the sword and attending upon matters of tribute. Then it commands to render tribute to whom tribute is due, and says, "Owe no man any thing; but to love one another; for he that loveth another hath fulfilled the law." Then he refers to the sixth, seventh, eighth, ninth, and tenth commandments, and says, "If there be any other commandment, it is briefly comprehended in this saying, namely, Thou shalt love thy neighbor as thyself."

There are other commandments of this same law to which Paul refers. Why, then, did he say, "If there be any other commandment, it is briefly comprehended in this saying, Thou shalt love thy neighbor as thyself"? There are the four commandments of the first table of this same law, — the commandments which say, "Thou shalt have no other gods before me; Thou shalt not make any graven image, or any likeness of any thing; Thou shalt not take the name of the Lord thy God in vain; Remember the Sabbath day to keep it holy." Then there is the other commandment in which are briefly comprehended all these, — "Thou shalt love the Lord thy God with all thy heart, and with all thy soul, and with all thy mind, and with all thy strength."

Paul knew full well of these commandments. Why, then, did he say, "If there be any other commandment, it is briefly comprehended in this saying, Thou shalt love thy neighbor as thyself"? *Answer.* — Because he was writing concerning the words of the Saviour which relate to our duties to civil government.

Our duties under civil government pertain solely to the government and to our fellow-men, because the powers of civil government pertain solely to men in their relations one to another, and to the government. But the Saviour's words in the same connection entirely separated that which pertains to God from that which pertains to civil government. The things which pertain to God are not to be rendered to civil government—to the powers that be; therefore Paul, although knowing full well that there were other commandments, said, "If there be any other commandment, it is briefly comprehended in this saying, Thou shalt love thy neighbor as thyself;" that is, if there be any other commandment which comes into the relation between man and civil government, it is comprehended in this saying, that he shall love his neighbor as himself; thus showing conclusively that the powers that be, though ordained of God, are so ordained simply in things pertaining to the relation of man with his fellow-men, and in those things alone.

Further, as in this divine record of the duties that men owe to the powers that be, there is no reference whatever to the first table of the law, it therefore follows that the powers that be, although ordained of God, have nothing whatever to do with the relations which men bear toward God

As the ten commandments contain the whole duty of man, and as in the scriptural enumerations of the duties that men owe to the powers that be, there is no mention of any of the things contained in the first table of the law, it follows that none of the duties enjoined in the first table of the law of God, do men owe to the powers that be; that is to say, again, that the powers that be, although ordained of God, are not ordained of God in anything pertaining to a single duty enjoined in any one of the first four of the ten commandments. These are

duties that men owe to God, and with these the powers
that be can of right have nothing to do, because Christ
has commanded to render unto God — not to Cæsar, nor
by Cæsar — that which is God's.

This is confirmed by other scriptures : —

"In the beginning of the reign of Jehoiakim, the son
of Josiah king of Judah, came this word unto Jeremiah
from the Lord, saying, Thus saith the Lord to me : Make
thee bonds and yokes, and put them upon thy neck, and
send them to the king of Edom, and to the king of
Moab, and to the king of the Ammonites, and to the
king of Tyrus, and to the king of Zidon, by the hand
of the messengers which come to Jerusalem unto Zedekiah
king of Judah, and command them to say unto their masters, Thus saith the Lord of hosts, the God of Israel :
Thus shall ye say unto your masters : I have made the
earth, the man and the beast that are upon the ground,
by my great power and by my outstretched arm, and
have given it unto whom it seemed meet unto me. And
now have I given all these lands into the hand of Nebuchadnezzar the king of Babylon, my servant ; and the
beasts of the field have I given him also to serve him.
And all nations shall serve him, and his son, and his
son's son, until the very time of his land come, and then
many nations and great kings shall serve themselves of
him. And it shall come to pass that the nation and
kingdom which will not serve the same Nebuchadnezzar
the king of Babylon, and that will not put their neck under
the yoke of the king of Babylon, that nation will I punish, saith the Lord, with the sword, and with the famine,
and with the pestilence, until I have consumed them by
his hand."

In this scripture it is clearly shown that the power
of Nebuchadnezzar, king of Babylon, was ordained of
God ; nor to Nebuchadnezzar alone, but to his son and
his son's son ; which is to say that the power of the
Babylonian empire, as an imperial power, was ordained
of God. Nebuchadnezzar was plainly called by the Lord,
" My servant," and the Lord says, " And now have I

given all these lands into the hand of Nebuchadnezzar the king of Babylon." He further says that whatever "nation and kingdom which will not serve the same Nebuchadnezzar the king of Babylon, and that will not put their neck under the yoke of the king of Babylon, that nation will I punish."

Now let us see whether this power was ordained of God in things pertaining to God. In the third chapter of Daniel we have the record that Nebuchadnezzar made a great image of gold, set it up in the plain of Dura, and gathered together the princes, the governors, the captains, the judges, the treasurers, the counselors, the sheriffs, and all the rulers of the provinces, to the dedication of the image ; and they stood before the image that had been set up. Then a herald from the king cried aloud : —

"To you it is commanded, O people, nations, and languages, that at what time ye hear the sound of the cornet, flute, harp, sackbut, psaltery, dulcimer, and all kinds of music, ye fall down and worship the golden image that Nebuchadnezzar the king hath set up ; and whoso falleth not down and worshipeth shall the same hour be cast into the midst of a burning fiery furnace."

In obedience to this command, all the people bowed down and worshiped before the image, except three Jews, Shadrach, Meshach, and Abed-nego. This disobedience was reported to Nebuchadnezzar, who commanded them to be brought before him, when he asked them if they had disobeyed his order intentionally. He himself then repeated his command to them.

These men knew that they had been made subject to the king of Babylon by the Lord himself. It had not only been prophesied by Isaiah (chap. 39), but by Jeremiah. At the final siege of Jerusalem by Nebuchadnezzar, the Lord through Jeremiah told the people to submit to the king of Babylon, and that whosoever would do it

3

it should be well with them ; whosoever would not do it, it should be ill with them. Yet these men, knowing all this, made answer to Nebuchadnezzar thus : —

"O Nebuchadnezzar, we are not careful to answer thee in this matter. If it be so, our God whom we serve is able to deliver us from the burning fiery furnace, and he will deliver us out of thine hand, O king. But if not, be it known unto thee, O king, that we will not serve thy gods, nor worship the golden image which thou hast set up."

Then these men were cast into the fiery furnace, heated seven times hotter than it was wont to be heated ; but suddenly Nebuchadnezzar rose up in haste and astonishment, and said to his counselors, "Did we not cast three men bound into the midst of the fire?" They answered, "True, O king." But he exclaimed, "Lo, I see four men loose, walking in the midst of the fire, and they have no hurt ; and the form of the fourth is like the Son of God." The men were called forth ; —

"Then Nebuchadnezzar spake and said, Blessed be the God of Shadrach, Meshach, and Abed-nego, who hath sent his angel and delivered his servants that trusted in him, and have changed the king's word, and yielded their bodies, that they might not serve nor worship any god, except their own God."

Here we have demonstrated the following facts : First, God gave power to the kingdom of Babylon ; second, he suffered his people to be subjected to that power ; third, he defended his people by a wonderful miracle from a certain exercise of that power. Does God contradict or oppose himself? — Far from it. What, then, does this show ? — It shows conclusively that this was an undue exercise of the power which God had given. By this it is demonstrated that the power of the kingdom of Babylon, although ordained of God, was not ordained unto any such purpose as that for which it was exercised ; and

that though ordained of God, it was not ordained to be
authority in things pertaining to God, or in things pertaining to men's consciences. And it was written for the
instruction of future ages, and for our admonition upon
whom the ends of the world are come.

Another instance: We read above that the power
of Babylon was given to Nebuchadnezzar, and his son,
and his son's son, and that all nations should serve Babylon until that time, and that then nations and kings
should serve themselves of him. Other prophecies show
that Babylon was then to be destroyed. Jer. 51:28 says
that the kings of the Medes, and all his land, with the
captains and rulers, should be prepared against Babylon
to destroy it. Isa. 21:2 shows that Persia (Elam) should
accompany Media in the destruction of Babylon. Isa.
45:1–4 names Cyrus as the leader of the forces, more
than a hundred years before he was born, and one hundred
and seventy-four years before the time. And of Cyrus,
the prophet said from the Lord, "I have raised him up
in righteousness, and I will direct all his ways; he shall
build my city, and he shall let go my captives, not for
price, nor reward, saith the Lord of hosts." Isa. 45:13.
But in the conquest of Babylon, Cyrus was only the
leader of the forces. The kingdom and rule were given
to Darius the Mede; for, said Daniel to Belshazzar, on
the night when Babylon fell, "Thy kingdom is divided,
and given to the Medes and Persians." Then the record
proceeds: "In that night was Belshazzar the king of the
Chaldeans slain. And Darius the Median took the kingdom." Of him we read in Dan. 11:1, the words of the
angel Gabriel to the prophet, "I, in the first year of Darius
the Mede, even I, stood to confirm and to strengthen him."

There can be no shadow of doubt, therefore, that the
power of Media and Persia was ordained of God. Darius
made Daniel prime minister of the empire. But a num-

ber of the presidents and princes, envious of the position
given to Daniel, attempted to undermine him.   After
earnest efforts to find occasion against him in matters pertaining to the kingdom, they were forced to confess that
there was neither error nor fault anywhere in his conduct.   Then said these men, "We shall not find any occasion against this Daniel, except we find it against
him concerning the law of his God."   They therefore
assembled together to the king, and told him that all the
presidents of the kingdom, and the governors, and the
princes, and the captains, had consulted together to establish a royal statute, and to make a decree that whoever should ask a petition of any god or man, except the
king, for thirty days, should be cast into the den of lions.
Darius, not suspecting their object, signed the decree.
Daniel knew that the decree had been made, and signed
by the king.   It was hardly possible for him not to know
it, being prime minister.   Yet notwithstanding his knowledge of the affair, he went into his chamber, and his windows being opened toward Jerusalem, he kneeled upon his
knees three times a day, and prayed and gave thanks before God, as he did aforetime.   He did not even close the
windows.   He paid no attention to the decree that had
been made, although it forbade his doing as he did, under
the penalty of being thrown to the lions.   He well understood that although the power of Media and Persia was
ordained of God, it was not ordained to interfere in matters of duty which he owed only to God.

As was to be expected, the men who had secured
the passage of the decree, found him praying and making supplications before his God.   They went at once to
the king and asked him if he had not signed a decree
that every man who should ask a petition of any god
or man within thirty days, except of the king, should
be cast into the den of lions.   The king replied that this

was true, and that, according to the law of the Medes and Persians, it could not be altered. Then they told him that Daniel did not regard the king, nor the decree that he had signed, but made his petition three times a day. The king realized in a moment that he had been entrapped ; but there was no remedy. Those who were pushing the matter, held before him the law, and said, "Know, O king, that the law of the Medes and Persians is, That no decree or statute which the king establisheth may be changed." Nothing could be done ; the decree, being law, must be enforced. Daniel was cast to the lions. In the morning the king came to the den and called to Daniel, and Daniel replied, "O king, live forever ; my God hath sent his angel, and hath shut the lions' mouths, that they have not hurt me : forasmuch as before him innocency was found in me ; and also before thee, O king, have I done no hurt."

Thus again God has shown that although the powers that be are ordained of God, they are not ordained to act in things that pertain to men's relation toward God. Christ's words are a positive declaration to that effect, and Rom. 13 : 1-9 is a further exposition of the principle.

Let us look a moment at this question from a common-sense point of view ; of course, all we are saying is common sense, but let us have this in addition : "When societies are formed, each individual surrenders certain rights, and as an equivalent for that surrender, has secured to him the enjoyment of certain others appertaining to his person and property, without the protection of which society cannot exist."

I have the right to protect my person and property from all invasions. Every other person has the same right ; but if this right is to be personally exercised in all cases by every one, then in the present condition of human nature, every man's hand will be against his neighbor. That is simple anarchy, and in such a condition of affairs society cannot exist. Now suppose a hundred of us are thrown together in a certain place where there is no established order ; each one has all the rights of any other one. But if each one is individually to exercise these rights of self-protection, he has the assurance of only that degree of protection which he alone can furnish to himself, which we have seen is exceedingly slight. Therefore all come together, and each surrenders to the whole body that individual right ; and in return for this surrender, he receives the power of all for his protection. He therefore receives the help of the other ninety-nine to protect himself from the invasion of his rights, and he is thus made many hundred times more secure in his rights of person and property than he is without this surrender.

But what condition of things can ever be conceived of among men that would justify any man in surrendering his right to believe ? What could he receive as an equivalent ? When he has surrendered his right to believe, he has virtually surrendered his right to think. When he surrenders his right to believe, he surrenders everything, and it is impossible for him ever to receive an equivalent ; he has surrendered his very soul. Eternal life depends upon believing on the Lord Jesus Christ, and the man who surrenders his right to believe, surrenders eternal life. Says the Scripture, "With the mind I myself serve the law of God." A man who surrenders his right to believe, surrenders God. Consequently, no man, no association or organization of men, can ever rightly ask of any man a surrender of his right to believe. Every man has the right, so far as organizations of men are concerned, to believe as he pleases ; and that right, so long as he is a Protestant, so long as he is a Christian, yes, so long as he is a man, he never can surrender, and he never will.

Another important question to consider in this connection is, How are the powers that be, ordained of God? Are they directly and miraculously ordained, or are they providentially so? We have seen by the Scripture that the power of Nebuchadnezzar as king of Babylon, was ordained of God. Did God send a prophet or a priest to anoint him king? or did he send a heavenly messenger, as he did to Moses and Gideon?—Neither. Nebuchadnezzar was king because he was the son of his father, who had been king. How did his father become king?—In 625 B. C., Babylonia was but a province of the empire of Assyria; Media was another. Both revolted, and at the same time. The king of Assyria gave Nabopolassar command of a large force, and sent him to Babylonia to quell the revolt, while he himself led other forces into Media, to put down the insurrection there. Nabopolassar did his work so well in Babylonia that the king of Assyria rewarded him with the command of that province, with the title of King of Babylon. Thus we see that Nabopolassar received his power from the king of Assyria. The king of Assyria received his from his father, Asshur-bani-pal; Asshur-bani-pal received his from his father, Esar-haddon; Esar-haddon received his from his father, Sennacherib; Sennacherib received his from his father, Sargon; and Sargon received his from the troops in the field, that is, from the people. Thus we see that the power of the kingdom of Babylon, and of Nebuchadnezzar the king, or of his son, or of his son's son, was simply providential, and came merely from the people.

Take, for example, Victoria, queen of Great Britain. How did she receive her power?—Simply by the fact that she was the first in the line of succession when William the Fourth died. Through one line she traces her royal lineage to William the Conqueror. But who was William the Conqueror?—He was a Norman chief who led his forces into England in 1066, and established his power there. How did he become a chief of the Normans?— The Normans made him so, and in that line it is clear that the power of Queen Victoria sprung only from the people.

Following the other line: The house that now rules Britain, represented in Victoria, is the house of Hanover. Hanover is a province of Germany. How came the house of Hanover to reign in England?— When Queen Anne died, the next in the line of succession was George of Hanover, who became king of England under the title of George the First. How did he receive his princely dignity?— Through his lineage, from Henry the Lion, son of Henry the Proud, who received the duchy of Saxony from Frederick Barbarossa, in 1156. Henry the Lion, son of Henry the Proud, was a prince of the house of Guelph, of Swabia. The father of the house of Guelph was a prince of the Alamanni who invaded the Roman empire, and established their power in what is now Southern Germany, and were the origin of what is now the German nation and empire. But who made this man a prince?— The savage tribes of Germany. So in this line also the royal dignity of Queen Victoria sprung from the people.

And besides all this, the imperial power of Queen Victoria as she now reigns is circumscribed — limited — by the people. It has been related, and has appeared in print, and although the story may not be true, it will serve to illustrate the point, that on one occasion, Gladstone, while prime minister and head of the House of Commons, took a certain paper to the queen to be signed. She did not exactly approve of it, and said she would not sign it. Gladstone spoke of the merit of the act, but the queen still declared she would not sign it. Gladstone replied, "Your Majesty *must* sign it." "*Must* sign!" exclaimed the queen; "*must* sign! Do you know who I am? I am the queen of England." Gladstone calmly replied, "Yes, Your Majesty, but I am the PEOPLE of England;" and she had to sign it. The people of England can command the queen of England; the power of the people of England is above that of the queen of England. She, as queen, is simply the representative of their power.' And if the people of England should choose to dispense with their expensive luxury of royalty, and turn their form of government into that of a republic, it would be but legitimate exercise of their right, and the government thus formed, the power thus established, would be ordained of God as much as that which now is, or as any could be.

Personal sovereigns in themselves are not those referred to in the words, "The powers that be are ordained of God." It is the governmental power of which the sovereign is the representative, and that sovereign receives his power from the people. Outside of the theocracy of Israel, there never has been a ruler on earth whose authority was not, primarily or ultimately, expressly or permissively, derived from the people. It is not particular sovereigns whose power is ordained of God, nor any particular form of government. *It is the genius of government itself.* The absence of government is anarchy. Anarchy is only governmental confusion. But says the Scripture, "God is not the author of confusion." God is the God of order. He has ordained order, and he has put within man himself that idea of government, of self-protection, which is the first law of nature, and which organizes itself into forms of one kind or another, wherever men dwell on the face of the earth. And it is for men themselves to say what shall be the form of government under which they shall dwell. One people has one form; another has another. This genius of civil order

springs from God ; its exercise within its legitimate sphere
is ordained of God ; and the Declaration of Independence
simply asserted the eternal truth of God, when it said :
"Governments derive their just powers from the consent
of the governed."   It matters not whether it be exercised
in one form of government or in another, the governmental power and order thus exercised is ordained of God.
If the people choose to change their form of government,
it is still the same power ; it is to be respected still,
because it is still ordained of God in its legitimate exercise, — in things pertaining to men and their relation to
their fellow-men ; but no power, whether exercised
through one form or another, is ordained of God to act
in things pertaining to God ; nor has it anything whatever to do with men's relations toward God.

In the previous chapter we have shown that the Constitution of the United States is the only form of government that has ever been on earth which is in harmony
with the principle announced by Christ, demanding of
men only that which is Cæsar's, and refusing to enter in
any way into the field of man's relationship to God. This
Constitution originated in the principles of the Declaration of Independence, and here we have found that the
Declaration of Independence, on this point, simply asserts
the truth of God.   The American people do not half ap-
preciate the value of the Constitution under which they
live.   They do not honor in any fair degree the noble men
who pledged their lives, their fortunes, and their sacred
honor, that these principles might be the heritage of posterity.   All honor to these noble men !   All integrity to
the principles of the Declaration of Independence !   All
allegiance to the Constitution as it is, which gives to
Cæsar all his due, and leaves men free to render to God
all that he, in his holy word, requires of them !

CHAPTER IV.

THE principles set forth in the three preceding chapters are the genuine principles of Jesus Christ. The United States Constitution as it is, with its total separation of religion and the State, is in perfect harmony with these principles. It is evident, therefore, that any attempt to introduce into our national Constitution any religion, even though it be, professedly, the Christian religion, would be subversive of the principles of Christ. Any such attempt would be anti-Christian, and would be fraught with the greatest danger that could threaten the liberties of men, and with the worst evils that could befall a nation. Such an attempt is not only being made, but is so far advanced as to make this a subject of the very first importance to every lover of Christianity or human rights.

The following resolution was offered in the United States Senate, May 25, 1888, by Senator Henry W. Blair, of New Hampshire. We present an exact copy : —

"50th CONGRESS, ⎱ S. R. 86.
1st SESSION. ⎰

" Joint Resolution, proposing an amendment to the Constitution of the United States respecting establishments of religion and free public schools.

" *Resolved by the Senate and House of Representatives of the United States of America in Congress assembled (two*

(43)

thirds of each House concurring therein), That the following amendment to the Constitution of the United States be, and hereby is, proposed to the States, to become valid when ratified by the legislatures of three fourths of the States, as provided in the Constitution : —

"ARTICLE.

"SECTION 1. No State shall ever make or maintain any law respecting an establishment of religion, or prohibiting the free exercise thereof.

"SEC. 2. Each State in this Union shall establish and maintain a system of free public schools adequate for the education of all the children living therein, between the ages of six and sixteen years, inclusive, in the common branches of knowledge, and in virtue, morality, and the principles of the Christian religion. But no money raised by taxation imposed by law, or any money or other property or credit belonging to any municipal organization, or to any State, or to the United States, shall ever be appropriated, applied, or given to the use or purposes of any school, institution, corporation, or person, whereby instruction or training shall be given in the doctrines, tenets, belief, ceremonials, or observances peculiar to any sect, denomination, organization, or society, being, or claiming to be, religious in its character ; nor shall such peculiar doctrines, tenets, belief, ceremonials, or observances be taught or inculcated in the free public schools.

"SEC. 3. To the end that each State, the United States, and all the people thereof, may have and preserve governments republican in form and in substance, the United States shall guaranty to every State, and to the people of every State and of the United States, the support and maintenance of such a system of free public schools as is herein provided.

"SEC. 4. That Congress shall enforce this article by legislation when necessary."

The adoption of any such amendment as this would be but the establishment of a national religion, and the enforcement of that religion upon all the States ; and would pledge the nation to an endless course of religious legislation **and religious** controversy. Upon their face the first two sections **of** this **proposed** amendment appear to be contradictory. The first **section declares** that "**no** State shall **ever m**ake or maintain **any** law respecting **an** establishment **of religion, or prohibiting** the free **exercise** thereof;" while the **first** sentence of the second **section** declares that "each State in the Union *shall establish* and *maintain* a system of free public schools, adequate **for the education** of all the children living therein, between **the** ages of six and sixteen years, inclusive, in the **common** branches of knowledge, and in virtue, morality, *and the principles of the Christian religion.*" That is **to say, no** State shall **ever** make or **maintain a law respecting the** establishment **of religion ; but every State in this** Union *shall make* and *maintain* laws establishing the principles of the *Christian* religion.

These **two sections are contradictory, or else** the first one **means only that** no State **shall make or** maintain any law **respecting** an establishment **of** religion *except at the dictation of the national power.* This last view seems to be the one contemplated in **the** amendment, **as the** third **section** plainly says that "the **United States shall guar**anty **to every** State, and **to the** people of **every State and of** the United **States, the** support and maintenance **of such a** system **of** free public **schools** as is herein **pro**vided." That **is to** say, the United States Government shall **either** compel each State to establish and maintain the principles of the Christian religion in **its** public schools, **or else the national** Government **will** do this itself. **This opens the broad question of the** centralization **of power, and of the limitations of the** national power **upon the** States, into **the discussion of which** we will not **enter.** Whatever bearing this **proposed** amendment may have upon those questions, there is one thing which is **certain beyond** all manner of doubt, and that is that **the**

direct result of the proposed amendment is the establishment of Christianity as the national religion of the United
States ; for —

1. It distinctly pledges the national power to the establishment and maintenance of the principles of the Christian religion.

2. It empowers Congress to legislate upon the subject
of the Christian religion, and to enforce by legislation the
teaching of the principles of that religion in all the public
schools in the nation.

3. If this proposed amendment should be adopted,
there must necessarily be a national decision declaring
just what are the principles of the Christian religion.
Then when that decision shall have been rendered, every
State and the people of every State will have to receive
from the nation, as the principles of the Christian religion, just those things which the nation shall have declared
to be the principles of the Christian religion, and which
the nation will have pledged itself to see taught in the
public schools of every State.   In other words, the people
of the United States will then have to receive their religion from the Government of the United States.

Therefore, if Senator Blair's proposed amendment to
the national Constitution does not provide for the establishment and maintenance of a national religion, then no
religion was ever nationally established or maintained in
this world.

Another important question is, How shall this national
decision as to what are the principles of the Christian religion, be made ?   It would seem that the second sentence of Section 2 makes provision for this.   It declares
that no "instruction or training shall be given in the doctrines, tenets, belief, ceremonials, or observances peculiar
to any sect, denomination, organization, or society, being,
or claiming to be, religious in its character ; nor shall

such peculiar doctrines, tenets, belief, ceremonials, or observances be taught or inculcated in the free public schools." As no religious doctrines, tenets, or belief can be taught in the schools except such as are common to all denominations of the Christian religion, it will follow inevitably that a national council of the churches will have to be officially called, to decide what are the principles common to all, and to establish a national creed, which shall be enforced and inculcated by national power in all the public schools in the United States.

This is confirmed by the author of the proposed amendment. In a letter to the secretary of the National Reform Association, Senator Blair says:—

"I believe that a text-book of instruction in the principles of virtue, morality, and of the Christian religion, can be prepared for use in the public schools, by the joint effort of those who represent every branch of the Christian church, both Protestant and Catholic, and also those who are not actively associated with either"

This virtually says that "by the joint effort of those who represent every branch of the Christian church, both Protestant and Catholic," there shall be framed a national creed which the United States Government shall adopt and enforce in all the public schools in the nation. Does anybody who has any acquaintance with history need to be shown the perfect parallel between this and the formation of that union of church and State in the fourth century, which developed the papacy and all the religious despotism and intolerance that has been witnessed in Europe and America from that time to this?

It was in this way precisely that the thing was worked in the fourth century. Constantine made Christianity the recognized religion of the Roman empire. Then it became at once necessary that there should be an imperial decision as to what form of Christianity should be the imperial religion. To effect this, an imperial council was necessary to formulate that phase of Christianity which was common to all. The Council of Nice was convened by imperial command, and an imperial creed was established, which was enforced by imperial power. That establishment of an imperial religion ended only in the imperious despotism of the papacy. And as surely as the complete establishment of the papacy followed, and grew out of, that imperial recognition of Christianity in the fourth century, just so surely will the complete establishment of a religious despotism after the living likeness of the papacy, follow, and grow out of, this national recognition of Christianity provided for in the Constitutional amendment proposed by Senator Blair, and which is now pending in Congress.

In proof of this, we have not only the logical deduction and the historical example, but in addition to these we have living, present facts. We mentioned above, Senator Blair's letter to the secretary of the National Reform Association. This letter was written in answer to an invitation to the senator to attend a meeting in Philadelphia in support of the proposed amendment. The initiative in bringing about this meeting was taken by the National Reform Association. This Association has been working for twenty-five years to secure an amendment to the national Constitution, making Christianity the established religion. Senator Blair's proposed amendment furnishes them just what they have so long wanted, and ever since he offered it, they have been diligently working to make it popular.

The *Christian Statesman*, published in Philadelphia, is the official organ of the Association, and in the issue of July 12, 1888, the editor says the amendment "should receive the strenuous support of all American Christians." In the issue of July 19, he says : —

"Senator Blair's proposed Constitutional amendment furnishes an admirable opportunity for making the ideas of the National Reform Association familiar to the minds of the people."

Then after mentioning "Christianity, the religion of the nation," and "the Bible, the text-book of our common Christianity in all the schools," he says: —

"These have been our watch-words in the discussions of a quarter of a century. And now these ideas are actually pending before the Senate of the United States, in the form of a joint resolution proposing their adoption as a part of the Constitution of the United States. Here is a great opportunity. Shall we boldly and wisely improve it?"

In the *Statesman* of July 26, 1888, Rev. J. C. K. Milligan, once a district secretary, and still a leading member of that Association, says to the editor:—

"Your editorial of July 12, on a Christian Constitutional amendment pending in the Senate, is most gratifying news to every Christian patriot. It seems too good to be true. It is too good to prevail without a long pull, a strong pull, and a pull all together on the part of its friends; but it is so good that it surely will have many friends who will put forth the necessary effort. True, the pending amendment has its chief value in one phrase, "the Christian religion;" but if it shall pass into our fundamental law, that one phrase will have all the potency of Almighty God, of Christ the Lord, of the Holy Bible, and of the Christian world, with it. By letters to senators and representatives in Congress, by petitions numerously signed and forwarded to them, by local, State, and national conventions held, and public meetings in every school district, such an influence can quickly be brought to bear as will compel our legislators to adopt the measure, and enforce it by the needed legislation. The Christian pulpits, if they would, could secure its adoption before the dog-days end. The National Reform Association, the *Christian Statesman*, and the secretaries in the

4

field are charged with this work, and will not be wanting
as leaders in the cause."

In the same paper of August 9, Rev. R. C. Wylie
praises the proposed amendment, because it would, if
adopted, give the National Reformers an advantage
which they have not now.   He says : —

"We would then have a vantage ground we have not
now. The leading objection that has been urged against
us will have lost its power.   That objection, which has
such a tender regard for the infidel conscience, will have
spent its force against this amendment, and will be no
more fit for use against us."

The charge of an intention to invade the rights of conscience has been the leading one against the National
Reform Association. But says Mr. Wylie, If this
amendment is carried, this charge will lie against the
amendment, and will spend itself there, while the National
Reformers will escape. This charge is justly made
against the National Reformers, for they distinctly affirm
that the civil power has the right to compel the consciences of men. And the admission that if the amendment were adopted the charge would then lie against that,
is a confession that the proposed amendment, if adopted,
will invade the rights of conscience. And that is the
truth. It will surely do so.

John Alexander, the father of the movement, who
gives five hundred dollars every year to help it forward,
and in his will has provided that the same amount shall
be paid every year from his estate until the movement
shall have proved a success, and who gives a thousand
dollars at times besides all this, in the *Christian Statesman* of Sept. 6, 1888, congratulated the Association on
the introduction of the Blair amendment, and said, "the
National Reform Association ought to spare no pains and

omit no effort which may promise to secure its adoption ;"
and further says : —

"Let us begin without delay the circulation of petitions (to be furnished in proper form by the Association),
and let an opportunity be given to all parts of the country to make up a roll of petitions so great that it will
require a procession of wheelbarrows to trundle the
mighty mass into the presence of the representatives of
the nation in the House of Congress. . . . Let a mass
convention of the friends of the cause be held in Washington, when the Blair resolution shall be under discussion, to accompany with its influence the presentation
of the petitions, and to take such other action as may be
deemed best to arouse the nation to a genuine enthusiasm
in behalf of our national Christianity."

This is how the Blair Constitutional amendment is
viewed by these people. Now let us see what they propose to do with it when they get it.

The *Christian Statesman* of Oct. 2, 1884, said : —

"Give all men to understand that this is a Christian
nation, and that, believing that without Christianity we
perish, we must maintain by all means our Christian character. Inscribe this character on our Constitution. Enforce upon all who come among us the laws of Christian
morality."

To enforce upon men the laws of Christian morality, is nothing else than an attempt to compel them to be
Christians, and does in fact compel them to be hypocrites.
It will be seen at once that this will be but to invade the
rights of conscience, and this, one of the vice-presidents of
the Association declares, civil power has the right to do.
Rev. David Gregg, D. D., now pastor of Park Street Church,
Boston, a vice-president of the National Reform Association, plainly declared in the *Christian Statesman* of June
5, 1884, that the civil power " has the right to command
the consciences of men."

Rev. M. A. Gault, a district secretary and a leading worker of the Association, says : —

" Our remedy for all these malefic influences, is to have the Government simply set up the moral law and recognize God's authority behind it, and lay its hand on any religion that does not conform to it."

Rev. E. B. Graham, also a vice-president of the Association, in an address delivered at York, Neb., and reported in the *Christian Statesman* of May 21, 1885, said : —

" We might add in all justice, If the opponents of the Bible do not like our Government and its Christian features, let them go to some wild, desolate land, and in the name of the Devil, and for the sake of the Devil, subdue it, and set up a government of their own on infidel and atheistic ideas ; and then if they can stand it, stay there till they die."

How much different is that from the Russian despotism ? In the *Century* for April, 1888, Mr. Kennan gave a view of the statutes of Russia on the subject of crimes against the faith, quoting statute after statute providing that whoever shall censure the Christian faith or the orthodox church, or the Scriptures, or the holy sacraments, or the saints, or their images, or the Virgin Mary, or the angels, or Christ, or God, shall be deprived of all civil rights, and exiled for life to the most remote parts of Siberia. This is the system in Russia, and it is in the direct line of the wishes of the National Reform Association, with this difference, however, that Russia is content to send dissenters to Siberia, while the National Reformers want to send them to the Devil, straight.

In a speech in a National Reform convention held in New York City, Feb. 26, 27, 1873, Jonathan Edwards, D. D., said : —

" We want State and religion, and we are going to have it. It shall be that so far as the affairs of State require religion, it shall be religion — the religion of Jesus Christ. The Christian oath and Christian morality shall have in this land 'an undeniable legal basis.' We use the word *religion* in its proper sense, as meaning a man's personal relation of faith and obedience to God."

Then according to their own definition, the National Reform Association intends that the State shall obtrude itself into every man's personal relation of faith and obedience to God.   Mr. Edwards proceeds : —

" Now, we are warned that to ingraft this doctrine upon the Constitution will be oppressive ; that it will infringe the rights of conscience ; and we are told that there are atheists, deists, Jews, and Seventh-day Baptists who would be sufferers under it."

He then defines the terms, *atheist, deist, Jew,* and *Seventh-day Baptist*, and counts them all atheists, as follows : —

" These all are, for the occasion, and so far as our amendment is concerned, one class. They use the same arguments and the same tactics against us. They must be counted together, which we very much regret, but which we cannot help. The first-named is the leader in the discontent and in the outcry — the atheist, to whom nothing is higher or more sacred than man, and nothing survives the tomb. It is his class. Its labors are almost wholly in his interest ; its success would be almost wholly his triumph. The rest are adjuncts to him in this contest. They must be named from him ; they must be treated as, for this question, one party."

What now are the rights of the National Reform classification of atheists? Mr. Edwards asks the question and answers it thus : —

" What are the rights of the atheist? I would tolerate him as I would tolerate a poor lunatic ; for in my view his mind is scarcely sound. So long as he does not rave, so long as he is not dangerous, I would tolerate him. I would tolerate him as I would a conspirator. The atheist is a dangerous man."

Let us inquire for a moment what are the rights of the atheist. So far as earthly governments are concerned, has not any man just as much right to be an atheist as any other man has to be a Christian? If not, why not? We wish somebody would tell. Has not any man just as much right to be an atheist as Jonathan Edwards has to be a Doctor of Divinity? Can you compel him to be anything else? But how long does Mr. Edwards propose to tolerate him?—"So long as he does not rave." A lunatic may be harmless, and be suffered to go about as he chooses; yet he is kept under constant surveillance, because there is no knowing at what moment the demon in him may carry him beyond himself, and he become dangerous. Thus the National Reformers propose to treat those who disagree with them. So long as dissenters allow themselves to be cowed down like a set of curs, and submit to be domineered over by these self-exalted despots, all may go well; but if a person has the principle of a man, and asserts his convictions as a man ought to, then he is "raving," then he becomes "dangerous," and must be treated as a raving, dangerous lunatic.

Next, dissenters are to be tolerated as conspirators are. A political conspirator is one who seeks to destroy the Government itself; he virtually plots against the life of every one in the Government; and in that, he has forfeited all claims to the protection of the Government or the regard of the people. And this is the way dissenters are to be treated by the National Reformers, when they shall have secured the power they want. And these are the men to whom Senator Blair's proposed Constitutional amendment is intensely satisfactory, as that which, if adopted, will assure them, in the end, that which they want.

Mr. Edwards proceeds : —

" Yes, to this extent I will tolerate the atheist ; but no_ _ more. Why should I ? The atheist does not tolerate me. He does not smile either in pity or in scorn upon my faith. He hates my faith, and he hates me for my faith."

Remember that these men propose to make this a Christian nation. These are they who propose themselves as the supreme expositors of Christian doctrine in this nation. What beautiful harmony there is between these words of Mr. Edwards and those of the sermon on the mount ! Did the Saviour say, Hate them that hate you ; despise them that will not tolerate you ; and persecute them that do not smile upon your faith ? Is that the sermon on the mount ?— It is *not* the sermon on the mount. Jesus said, " Love your enemies ; bless them that curse you, do good to them that hate you, and pray for them which despitefully use you, and persecute you ; that ye may be the children of your Father which is in heaven." But this National Reform style of Christianity would have it : " Hate your enemies ; oppress them that hate you ; and persecute them who will not smile, either in pity or in scorn, upon your faith, that you may be the true children of the National Reform party ; " and that is what you will be, if you do it.

But Mr. Edwards has not yet finished displaying his tolerant ideas ; he says : —

" I can tolerate difference and discussion ; I can tolerate heresy and false religion ; I can debate the use of the Bible in our common schools, the taxation of church property, the propriety of chaplaincies and the like, but there are some questions past debate. *Tolerate atheism, sir? There is nothing out of hell that I would not tolerate as soon!* The atheist may live, as I have said ; but, God helping us, the taint of his destructive creed shall not defile any of the civil institutions of all this fair land !

Let us repeat, atheism and Christianity are contradictory terms. They are incompatible systems. *They cannot dwell together on the same continent!*" *

Worse than Russia again! Russia will suffer dissenters to dwell on the same continent with her, though it be in the most remote part of Siberia. But these men to whom Senator Blair's religious amendment is so satisfactory, propose to outdo even Russia, and not suffer dissenters to dwell on the same continent with them. In view of these statements of men now living, and actively working for this proposed amendment, is it necessary for us to say that Senator Blair's religious amendment to the Constitution is directly in the line of a religious despotism more merciless than that of Russia, and paralleled only by that of the papacy in the supremacy of its power?

But as though this were not enough, and as though their tolerant intentions were not sincere enough, they propose in addition to all this to join hands with the Catholic Church and enlist her efforts in their work. The *Christian Statesman* of Dec. 11, 1884, said : —

"Whenever they [the Roman Catholics] are willing to co-operate in resisting the progress of political atheism, we will gladly join hands with them."

What does Pope Leo XIII. command all Catholics to do ? — This : —

"All Catholics should do all in their power to cause the constitutions of States, and legislation, to be modeled on the principles of the true church."

The National Reformers are doing precisely what the pope has commanded all Catholics to do, and why should n't

---

* Let not the reader think that because this was spoken fifteen years ago, it is now out of date; for that Association to-day advertises and sells this speech as representative National Reform literature, and the pamphlet in which it is contained can be had by sending twenty-five cents to the *Christian Statesman*, 1520 Chestnut street, Philadelphia, Pa.

they gladly join hands with them? And we may rest assured that Rome will accept the National Reform proffer just as soon as the influence of that Association becomes of sufficient weight to be profitable to her. Senator Blair's proposed amendment is a direct play into the hands of the papacy.·

Thus it is clearly demonstrated that Senator Blair's proposed Constitutional amendment, if adopted, will only open the way to the establishment of a religious despotism in this dear land, and that this is the very use those who are most in favor of it intend to make of it. And to favor that amendment is to favor a religious despotism.

But the question may be asked, whether we mean soberly to say that an association that sets forth such abominable propositions can have any influence at all in this enlightened age, or can be counted worthy of recognition, or of the fellowship of respectable people? Well, let us see.

Senator Blair is a respectable personage, and in the letter before mentioned he said to the secretary of that Association : —

"I earnestly trust that your movement may become strong, general, in fact, all-pervading ; for the time has fully come when action is imperative and further delay is most dangerous."

But whether any delay could possibly be more dangerous than would be the success of this movement, we leave the reader to decide.

Joseph Cook, the Boston Monday lecturer, is a vice-president of that Association. President Seelye, of Amherst College, is also one of the vice-presidents. Bishop Huntington, of New York, is another. The president of the W. C. T. U. is another ; and so is Mrs. J. C. Bateham, of the National Union, and Mrs. Woodbridge, of the same organization. Miss Mary A. West, editor of the *Union Signal;* Mrs. Hoffman, president of the Missouri Union ;

Mrs. Lathrap, president of the Michigan Union; Mrs. Sibley, of the Georgia Union; Mrs. J. Ellen Foster, of the Iowa Union, — all these are upon the printed list of vice-presidents of that Association for the present year, and all these are eminently respectable people. They are people of influence. In a letter dated Cliff Seat, Ticonderoga, N. Y., Aug. 6, 1887, Joseph Cook hopes to aid the movement "by voice and pen."

In the published reports of the National Reform Association for the years 1886-87, appears the following suggestion, made in 1885, on the relationship between the National W. C. T. U. and the National Reform Association : —

"Miss Francis E. Willard, president of the W. C. T. U., suggested the creation of a special department of its already manifold work, for the promotion of Sabbath observance, *co-operating with the National Reform Association.* The suggestion was adopted at the national convention in St. Louis, and the department was placed in the charge of Mrs. J. C. Bateham, of Ohio, as national superintendent. Mrs. Bateham has since, with her own cordial assent, been made one of the vice-presidents of the National Reform Association."

Again : —

"It was your secretary's privilege this year again to attend the national convention. A place was kindly given for an address in behalf of the National Reform Association, and thanks were returned by a vote of the convention. A resolution was adopted expressing gratitude to the National Association, for the advocacy of a suitable acknowledgment of the Lord Jesus Christ in the fundamental law of this professedly Christian nation."

And again : —

"In the series of monthly readings for the use of local unions as a responsive exercise, prepared or edited by Miss Willard, the reading for last July [1886] was on 'God in Government ;' that for August was 'Sabbath Observance' (prepared by Mrs. Bateham), and that for September, 'Our National Sins.' Touching the first and last named readings, your secretary had correspondence with their editor before they appeared. A letter has been prepared to W. C. T. U. workers and speakers, asking them in their public addresses to refer to and plead for the Christian principles of civil government. The president of the National Union allows us to say that this letter is sent with her sanction, and by her desire."

From the *Christian Statesman* of Nov. 15, 1888, we copy the following from a report of labor by Secretary M. A. Gault :—

"The four weeks I spent recently in the eighth Wisconsin district, lecturing under the auspices of the W. C. T. U., were among the most pleasant weeks since I went into the lecture field. The weather was unusually fine, and there were but very few meetings in which everything was not in apple-pie order. Ladies wearing the significant white ribbon met me at the train, and took me often to the most elegant home in the town. . . . The W. C. T. U. affords the best facilities for openings for such workers, more than any other organization. It is in sympathy with the movement to enthrone Christ in our Government. The eighth district W. C. T. U., at Augusta, Wis., Oct. 2, 3, and 4, passed this resolution : —

"'*Whereas*, God would have all men honor the Son, even as they honor the Father ; and, —

"'*Whereas*, The civil law which Christ gave from Sinai is the only perfect law, and the only law that will secure the rights of all classes ; therefore, —

"'*Resolved*, That civil government should recognize Christ as the moral Governor, and his law as the standard of legislation.'

"It is significant of how the heart of this great organization is beating, when such a resolution was passed without a dissenting voice by a district convention representing fifteen counties."

What more is necessary to show that the National Reform Association has secured the closest possible alliance with the W. C. T. U.? The national convention of the W. C. T. U. in 1888, by resolution indorsed the proposed Blair amendment as deserving their "earnest and united support."

But more than this, the purpose of the two associations, as officially declared, is the same. The National Reform Association is set for the turning of this Government into a theocracy, and the W. C. T. U. monthly reading for September, 1886, said the same thing, thus : —

"A true theocracy is yet to come, and the enthronement of Christ in law and law-makers ; hence I pray devoutly, as a Christian patriot, for the ballot in the hands of women, and rejoice that the National Woman's Christian Temperance Union has so long championed this cause." •

Again, the National Reform Association proposes to turn this Government into a kingdom of Christ, and the W. C. T. U., in national convention, 1887, said : —

"The Woman's Christian Temperance Union, local, State, national, and world-wide, has one vital, organic thought, one all-absorbing purpose, one undying enthusiasm, and that is that Christ shall be *this world's king;* — yea, verily, THIS WORLD'S KING in its realm of cause and effect, — king of its courts, its camps, its commerce, — king of its colleges and cloisters, — king of its customs and constitutions. . . . The kingdom of Christ must enter the realm of law through the gate-way of politics."

In conformity with this idea, the National Reformers have bestowed upon the Saviour the title of "The Divine Politician." Christ himself said, "My kingdom is not of this world." These two organizations declare that Christ *shall be* this world's king. There is not the slightest danger of mistake, therefore, in saying that the whole National Reform scheme, including Senator Blair's proposed amendment to the Constitution and the theocratical workings of the W. C. T. U., is *anti*-Christian.

We believe that not one tenth of the great body of
the W. C. T. U. have any idea of what this alliance with
the National Reform Association amounts to.   There are
none who have more respect or more good wishes for the
W. C. T. U., in the line of its legitimate work, than have
we.   We are heartily in favor of union, of temperance
union, of Christian temperance union, and of woman's
Christian temperance union; but we are *not* in favor
of any kind of political Christian temperance union,
nor of theocratical temperance union.   Would that the
W. C. T. U. would stick to their text, and work for
Christian temperance by Christian means!   The Iowa
Union has done itself the credit to separate from the
political workings of the National Union.   It ought to
go a step farther, and separate from the theocratical
workings of the National Union, also; and all the rest
of that body would do well to protest against both the
political and the theocratical workings of its present
leadership, and especially against the Union's any longer
being made a tool of the National Reform Association.
By means of the W. C. T. U., that Association is having
a thousand times as much influence as it could have if
left to itself to make its own way.

The National W. C. T. U. of 1888, resolved that, —

"Christ and his gospel, as universal king and code,
should be sovereign in our Government and political
affairs."

Well, let us try it.   Suppose the gospel were adopted
as the code of this Government.   It is the duty of every
court to act in accordance with its code.   There is a
statute in that code which says,—

"If thy brother trespass against thee, rebuke him; and
if he repent, forgive him.   And if he trespass against
thee seven times in a day, and seven times in a day turn
again to thee, saying, I repent, thou shalt forgive him."

Remember, they have resolved that this shall be the code in our Government. Suppose, then, a man steals a horse. He is arrested, tried, and found guilty. He says, "I repent." "Thou shalt forgive him," says the code, and the Government must conform to the code. He is released, and repeats the act ; is again arrested and found guilty. He says, "I repent." "Thou shalt forgive him." And if he repeats the offense seven times in a day, and seven times in a day turns to the court, saying, "I repent," the Government must forgive him, for so says that which the Woman's Christian Temperance Union has resolved should be the Governmental code.

It will be seen in an instant that any such system would be destructive of civil government. This is not saying anything against the Bible, nor against its principles. It is only illustrating the absurd perversion of its principles by these people who want to establish a system of religious legislation here. God's government is moral, and he has made provision for maintaining his government with the forgiveness of transgression. But he has made no such provision for civil government, and no such provision can be made. No such provision can be made, and civil government be maintained. The Bible reveals God's method of saving those who sin against his moral government ; civil government is man's method of preserving order, and has nothing to do with sin, nor the salvation of sinners. Civil government arrests a man and finds him guilty. If before the penalty is executed, he repents, God forgives him ; but the government executes the penalty, and it ought to.

Nor is this the only ally of the National Reform Association. The Third-party Prohibition party is another confederate in this attack upon the Constitution. Geo. W. Baine is a vice-president of that Association. And opposition to church and State was hissed and yelled down in the State Prohibition convention held in San Francisco in 1888; and that same convention adopted a platform recognizing the Lord as supreme Ruler, "to whose laws all human laws should conform."

Sam Small was secretary of the national Prohibition convention held at Indianapolis in 1888, and, as reported in a revival sermon preached in Kansas City, January, 1888, what he wants to see is this :—

"I want to see the day come when the church shall be the arbiter of all legislation, State, national, and municipal; when the great churches of the country can come together harmoniously, and issue their edict, and the legislative powers will respect it, and enact it into laws."

What more was the papacy ever than that? What more did it ever claim to be? What more could it have been?

Sam Jones is another ardent Third-party Prohibitionist. In the latter part of July, 1888, he preached in Windsor, Canada, to an audience composed mostly of Americans, who went over there to hear him. Here is one of his devout, elegantly refined, and intensely instructive passages : —

"Now I tell you, I think we are running the last political combat on the lines we have been running them on. It is between the Republicans and the Democrats, this contest, and it is the last the Republicans will make in America. The Democrats are going in overwhelmingly. Four years from now the Prohibition element will break the solid South. The issue then will be, God or no God, drunkenness or sobriety, Sabbath or no Sabbath, heaven or hell. That will be the issue. Then we will wipe up the ground with the Democratic party, and let God rule America from that time on."

And this the *Christian Statesman* inserts under the heading, "The National Reform Movement." It is very appropriately placed. It is a worthy addition to the literature of the National Reform movement.

On the way home from the Indianapolis convention, a
National Reformer, and a Third-party Prohibitionist, who
is a prominent speaker, were riding together in the railway car. A personal acquaintance of the writer sat in
the next seat to them. The National Reformer said that
the Prohibition party did not make enough of National
Reform principles ; the Prohibitionist replied : —

"We are just as much in favor of those principles as
you are ; but the time has not yet come to make them so
prominent as you wish. But you help put us into power,
and we will give you all you want."

Thus the Third-party Prohibition party is but another
ally of the National Reform Association.

When it is seen that this legislation is the first step toward the establishment of a religious despotism modeled
upon the principles of the papacy, and when this legislation is supported by such men as Joseph Cook, President
Seelye, Bishop Huntington, and the others named ; by
the W. C. T. U., and the Third-party Prohibition party,—
is it not time that somebody should say something in behalf of our Constitution as it is, and of the rights of men
under it ?

CHAPTER V.

THE proposed religious amendment to the national Constitution, introduced into the United States Senate by Senator Blair, is not the only attempt that is being made to commit Congress to a course of religious legislation. The proposed religious amendment to the Constitution was introduced May 25, 1888, but on May 21, 1888, the same Senator had introduced the following bill, which was read twice and referred to the Committee on Education and Labor.

"50th CONGRESS, } S. 2983.
   1st SESSION. }

" A Bill to secure to the people the enjoyment of the first day of the week, commonly known as the Lord's day, as a day of rest, and to promote its observance as a day of religious worship.

" *Be it enacted by* **the Senate and House** *of Representatives of the United* **States of America in** *Congress assembled,* That **no** person, or corporation, or the agent, servant, or employee of any person or corporation, shall **perform** or authorize to be performed any secular **work, labor, or** business **to the** disturbance of others, works **of necessity,** mercy, **and humanity excepted ; nor shall any person** engage in **any** play, **game, or amusement, or recreation,** to the disturbance **of others, on the first day of the week,** commonly known **as the Lord's day, or** during any part thereof, in **any** territory, district, vessel, or place subject to the **exclusive** jurisdiction of the United States ; nor shall **it be** lawful for any person **or** corporation to receive

5   (65)

pay for labor or service performed or rendered in violation of this section.

"SEC. 2. That no mails or mail matter shall hereafter be transported in time of peace over any land postal-route, nor shall any mail matter be collected, assorted, handled, or delivered during any part of the first day of the week: *Provided*, That whenever any letter shall relate to a work of necessity or mercy, or shall concern the health, life, or decease of any person, and the fact shall be plainly stated upon the face of the envelope containing the same, the postmaster-general shall provide for the transportation of such letter.

"SEC. 3. That the prosecution of commerce between the States and with the Indian tribes, the same not being work of necessity, mercy, or humanity, by the transportation of persons or property by land or water in such way as to interfere with or disturb the people in the enjoyment of the first day of the week, or any portion thereof, as a day of rest from labor, the same not being labor of necessity, mercy, or humanity, or its observance as a day of religious worship, is hereby prohibited ; and any person or corporation, or the agent, servant, or employee of any person or corporation who shall willfully violate this section, shall be punished by a fine of not less than ten nor more than one thousand dollars, and no service performed in the prosecution of such prohibited commerce shall be lawful, nor shall any compensation be recoverable or be paid for the same.

"SEC. 4. That all military and naval drills, musters, and parades, not in time of active service or immediate preparation therefor, of soldiers, sailors, marines, or cadets of the United States, on the first day of the week, except assemblies for the due and orderly observance of religious worship, are hereby prohibited ; nor shall any unnecessary labor be performed or permitted in the military or naval service of the United States on the Lord's day.

"SEC. 5. That it shall be unlawful to pay or to receive payment or wages in any manner for service rendered, or for labor performed, or for the transportation of persons or property, in violation of the provisions of this act, nor shall any action lie for the recovery thereof, and when so paid, whether in advance or otherwise, the same may be recovered back by whoever shall first sue for the same.

"Sec. 6. That labor or service performed and rendered on the first day of the week in consequence of accident, disaster, or unavoidable delays in making the regular connections upon postal-routes and routes of travel and transportation, the preservation of perishable and exposed property, and the regular and necessary transportation and delivery of articles of food in condition for healthful use, and such transportation for short distances from one State, district, or Territory into another State, district, or Territory as by local laws shall be declared to be necessary for the public good, shall not be deemed violations of this act, but the same shall be construed so far as possible to secure to the whole people rest from toil during the first day of the week, their mental and moral culture, and the religious observance of the Sabbath day."

The first section of this bill is contrary to the word of Christ. In enjoining the observance of the Lord's day, it demands that men shall render to Cæsar that which is the Lord's. But Christ said, "Render therefore to *Cæsar* the things which are Cæsar's; and unto God the things that are *God's*." That which is the Lord's is not to be rendered to Cæsar, but to the Lord. Cæsar is civil government; therefore, we are not to render to civil government that which is the Lord's; with that which is the Lord's Cæsar has nothing to do. Consequently no civil government can ever of right have anything to do, in legislative capacity, with the Lord's day. Senator Blair's bill, in legislating upon that which pertains to the Lord, plainly sets itself against the word of Christ, and is, therefore, anti-Christian.

Again, this section declares that no person shall do any work, nor "engage in any play, game, or amusement, or recreation, to the disturbance of others, on the first day of the week, commonly known as the Lord's day, or during any part thereof." This leaves it entirely with the other man to say whether that which you do disturbs him; and that is only to make every man's action on Sunday subject to the whim or caprice of his neighbor. And

everybody knows that it requires a very slight thing to
make a man an offender in the eyes of one who has a
spite or a prejudice against him. At the Illinois State
Sunday-law convention for 1888 (Nov 20, 21), Dr. R.
O. Post, of Springfield, made a speech on the subject of
"Sunday Recreation," in which he laid down the following rule on the subject : —

"There is no kind of recreation that is proper or profitable on Sunday, outside of the home or the sanctuary."

Only let such a law as is embodied in this bill of
Senator Blair's, be of force where R. O. Post, D. D., is, and
any kind of recreation outside of the home or the
sanctuary would be sure to disturb him, and the one engaged in the recreation could be arrested and prosecuted
But, it may be argued, that no judge or jury would uphold any such prosecution. That is not at all certain, as
we shall yet see ; but whether or not it is so, it is certain
that if your neighbor should say that what you did disturbed him, under such a law as that he could have you
arrested, and put to the inconvenience and expense of
defending yourself before the court. In 1887 the city of
San Francisco, Cal., had an ordinance on another subject
that embodied the very principle of this clause of the Blair
Sunday bill. It read as follows : —

"No person shall in any place indulge in conduct having a tendency to annoy persons passing or being upon
the public highway, or upon adjacent premises."

It is easy to see that the principle of this ordinance is
identical with that of the clause in the first section of the
Blair bill, which forbids anything "to the disturbance of
others."

While that San Francisco ordinance was in force, a
man by the name of Ferdinand Pape was distributing
some circulars on the street, which "annoyed" some-

body. He was arrested. He applied to the Superior Court for a writ of *habeas corpus*, claiming that the offense charged against him did not constitute a crime, and that the ordinance making such action an offense was invalid and void, because it was unreasonable and uncertain. The report of the case says : —

"The writ was made returnable before Judge Sullivan, and argued by Henry Hutton in behalf of the imprisoned offender. Disposing of the question, the Judge gave quite a lengthy written opinion, in which he passed a somewhat severe criticism upon the absurdity of the contested ordinance, and discharged Pape from custody. Said the Judge : —

"'If the order be law, enforceable by fine and imprisonment, it is a crime to indulge in any conduct, however innocent and harmless in itself, and however unconsciously done, which has a tendency to annoy other persons. The rival tradesman who passes one's store with an observant eye as to the volume of business, is guilty of a crime, because the very thought of rivalry and reduction of business has a tendency to annoy. The passing of the most lenient creditor has a tendency to annoy, because it is a reminder of obligations unfulfilled. The passing of a well-clad, industrious citizen, bearing about him the evidences of thrift, has a tendency to annoy the vagabond, whose laziness reduces him to a condition of poverty and discontent. The importunities of the newsboy who endeavors with such persistent energy to dispose of his stock, has a tendency to annoy the prominent citizen who has already read the papers, or who expects to find them at his door as he reaches home. He who has been foiled in an attempted wrong upon the person or property of another, finds a tendency to annoy in the very passing presence of the person whose honesty or ingenuity has circumvented him. And so instances might be multiplied indefinitely in which the most harmless and inoffensive conduct has a tendency to annoy others. If the language of the ordinance defines a criminal offense, it sets a very severe penalty of liberty and property upon conduct lacking in the essential element of criminality.

"'But it may be said that courts and juries will not use the instrumentality of this language to set the seal of condemnation on unoffending citizens, and to unjustly deprive them of their liberty and brand them as criminals. The law countenances no such dangerous doctrine, countenances no principle so subversive of liberty, as that the life or liberty of a subject should be made to depend upon the whim or caprice of judge or jury, by exercising a discretion in determining that certain conduct does or does not come within the inhibition of a criminal action. The law should be engraved so plainly and distinctly on the legislative tables that it can be discerned alike by all subjects of the commonwealth, whether judge upon the bench, juror in the box, or prisoner at the bar. Any condition of the law which allows the test of criminality to depend on the whim or caprice of judge or juror, savors of tyranny. The language employed is broad enough to cover conduct which is clearly within the Constitutional rights of the citizen. It designates no border-line which divides the criminal from the non-criminal conduct. Its terms are too vague and uncertain to lay down a rule of conduct. In my judgment, the portion of the ordinance here involved is uncertain and unreasonable.'"

This decision applies with full force to Senator Blair's proposed national Sunday law. Under that law, all that would be necessary to subject any person to a criminal prosecution, would be for him to engage in any sort of play, game, amusement, or recreation on Sunday; because the National Reformers are as much in favor of this Sunday law as they are in favor of the Blair religious amendment to the Constitution, and there are many of those rigid National Reformers who would be very much "disturbed" by any amusement or recreation indulged in on Sunday, however innocent it might be in itself. And it is left entirely to the whim or the caprice of the "disturbed" one, or of the judge or jury, to say whether the action really has or has not disturbed him.

The California decision is, that such a statute "sets a very severe penalty of liberty and property upon conduct lacking in the essential element of criminality." California courts "countenance no such dangerous doctrine, countenance no principle so subversive of liberty," or which so "savors of tyranny," as that which is embodied in the Blair Sunday bill.

Section 4 is directly in the line of Constantine's Sunday legislation. He, however, went a step farther, and caused his soldiers to parade expressly for worship on Sunday, and wrote out a prayer which he had them all repeat at a given signal. Something like this might appropriately follow, should this bill become a law ; because, as religious observance and religious worship are the objects of the bill, why should not the soldiers be required to pray on Sunday as well as otherwise to observe the day religiously ?

We shall not undertake to comment on every section of the bill, but Section 5 deserves to be particularly noticed. This section provides that if any person works for any other person on Sunday, and receives payment for it at any time, then any person in the wide world, except the parties concerned, can enter suit, and recover the money so paid. If you work for me on Sunday, and I pay you for it, then the first man that finds it out can sue you and get the money. That is what the bill says. When wages are paid for Sunday work, "whether in advance or otherwise, the same may be recovered back by *whoever* shall *first* sue for the same." *Whoever* is a universal term. Therefore, this bill deliberately proposes that when any man who is subject to the exclusive jurisdiction of the United States, receives payment for work done on Sunday, except for work of necessity or mercy, he may be sued for that money by whoever first learns that he has received it, and that person shall get the money.

To think that any such legislation as is embodied in this section should ever be thought of by any sane person, is sufficiently astonishing; but that it should not only have been thought of, but should have been embodied in a bill, and soberly introduced into the United States Senate, is simply astounding. It almost surpasses belief. But here are the facts which demonstrate that such things have been done in this land of liberty, in this year of the nineteenth century. When the time of a United States senator is employed in such legislation as that, then whose liberties are secure?

The last section shows the object of the entire bill; and that is, " to secure to the whole people rest, . . . and the religious observance of the Sabbath day." No one, therefore, need attempt to evade the force of objections against this bill by saying that it is not the religious, but the *civil*, observance of the day that is required ; because it is plainly declared in the bill itself, that it is not only to secure rest to all the people, but that it is also to secure the *religious* observance of the Sabbath day. There is not a single reference in the bill to any such thing as the civil observance of the day. The word *civil* is not used in the bill. It is a religious bill wholly. The title of the bill declares that its object is to secure to the people the enjoyment of the Lord's day as a day of rest, "and to promote its observance as a day of *religious worship*." The first section defines the Lord's day; the second section refers to the day as one of worship and rest ; the third section refers to it as a day of religious worship ; the fourth section refers to its observance as that of religious worship ; and the sixth section plainly declares, what is apparent throughout, that the object of the bill is "to secure to the whole people rest, . . . and the *religious* observance of the Sabbath day," on the first day of the week.

It is the religious observance of the day that its promoters, from one end of the land to the other, have in view. In the Washington Sunday convention, Dec. 12, 1888, Dr. Crafts said : —

" Taking religion out of the day, takes the rest out."

In the " Boston Monday Lectures," 1887, Joseph Cook, lecturing on the subject of Sunday laws, said : —

" The experience of centuries shows, however, that you will in vain endeavor to preserve Sunday as a day of rest, unless you preserve it as a day of worship. Unless Sabbath observance be *founded upon religious reasons*, you will not long maintain it at a high standard on the basis of economic and physiological and political considerations only."

And in the Illinois State Sunday convention held in Elgin, Nov. 8, 1887, Dr. W. W. Everts declared Sunday to be " the test of all religion."

Sunday is a religious institution wholly ; Sunday legislation, wherever found, is religious legislation solely ; and as we have seen, Senator Blair's Sunday bill does not pretend to be anything else than religious legislation. Being therefore as it is, religious legislation, it is clearly unconstitutional. In proof of this, we submit the following considerations : —

All the powers of Congress are delegated powers. It has no other power ; it cannot exercise any other. Article X. of Amendments to the Constitution expressly declares that, —

" The powers not delegated to the United States by the Constitution, nor prohibited by it to the States, are reserved to the States respectively, or to the people."

In all the powers thus delegated to Congress, there is no hint of any power to legislate upon any religious question, or in regard to the observance of any religious institution or rite. Therefore, Senator Blair's Sunday bill, being a religious bill, is unconstitutional ; and any legislation with regard to it will be unconstitutional. More

than this, Sunday being a religious institution, any legislation by Congress in regard to its observance, will be
unconstitutional as long as the United States Constitution shall remain as it now is. Nor is this all. The
Nation has not been left in doubt as to whether the fail- ·
ure to delegate this power was or was not intentional.
The first Amendment to the Constitution, in declaring
that, " Congress shall make no law respecting an establishment of religion, or prohibiting the free exercise
thereof," shows that the failure to delegate such power
was intentional, and makes the intention emphatic by.
absolutely prohibiting Congress from exercising any
power with regard to religion. It is impossible to frame
a law on the subject of religion that will not in some way
prohibit the free exercise of religion. Therefore the first
Amendment to the Constitution absolutely prohibits Congress from ever making any law with regard to any
religious subject, or the observance of any religious rite
or institution. Senator Blair's bill, being a religious bill,
is shown by this second count to be unconstitutional.

The National Reformers know and have been contending for twenty-five years that for Congress to make any
Sunday laws would be unconstitutional. Yet the National
Reform Association is one of the most prominent agencies
in urging forward Senator Blair's national Sunday bill.
And this only shows that they are willing to resort to
unconstitutional means to secure their coveted power,
and to accomplish their purposes. As for Dr. Crafts and
his fellow-workers, the W. C. T. U., etc., whether or not
they know it to be unconstitutional, we do not know.
Whether they would care, even though they did know,
we are not prepared to say, for this reason : In the an-
nouncements of the Washington national Sunday convention, Dec. 11–13, 1888, it had been stated that the
church in which the convention was to meet would be

festooned with the names of six millions of petitioners; but at the very beginning of the first meeting, it was stated that there were *fourteen* millions of them. A question was sent up asking how the number could have grown so much larger so suddenly. Mrs. Bateham was recalled to the platform to answer the question, and when she answered it, the cause of such a sudden and enormous growth was explained by the fact that Cardinal Gibbons had written a letter indorsing the Blair bill, and solely upon the strength of his name, seven million two hundred thousand Catholics were counted as *petitioners.*

This was not an entire answer to the question, because the Cardinal's letter did not authorize any such use of it as they had made, at least so much of it as was made public did not. The whole of the letter was not made public, because, Dr. Crafts said, it was for the Senate Committee. But so much of it as was read merely referred to the action of the Baltimore Council in commanding a stricter observance of Sunday, and said : —

"I am most happy to add my name to those of the millions of others who are laudably contending against the violation of the Christian Sabbath by unnecessary labor, and who are endeavoring to promote its decent and proper observance by judicious legislation."

This was all. He said, "I am happy to add *my name,*" etc. He did not say that he added, or that he wished to add, seven million two hundred thousand others with his name, or in his name. But the overweening anxiety of these *Christian* Protestant (?) Sunday-law workers for petitions, was so great that, without a twinge, they could and did multiply *one* Catholic name into seven million two hundred thousand *and one.* Yet this was not so much to be wondered at, because the same principle had been acted upon before throughout the country, and when five hundred petitioners could be made out of *one* hundred, and two hundred and forty *thousand* out of two hundred and forty, it was perfectly easy and entirely consistent to make seven million two hundred thousand and one out of *one*.

This thing was perfectly consistent also with the principle in another point. The petition read : " We, the undersigned, *adult* residents of the United States, *twenty-one years of age or more*, hereby petition," etc. In counting these seven million two hundred thousand petitioners in behalf of the Sunday law, they thereby certified that all these were Catholics " twenty-one years of age or more." But there was not a man in that convention, and there is not a woman in the Woman's Christian Temperance Union, who does not know that there are not that many Catholics in the United States "twenty-one years of age or more." They virtually certified that all the Catholics in the United States are "twenty-one years of age or more," for they distinctly announced that "all the Roman Catholics" were petitioning for the Sunday law. But when they had virtually certified the same thing of the Protestant churches throughout the country, why should they not go on and swing in "all the Roman Catholics" in the same way? They could do the one just as honestly as they could do the other. When men and women professing themselves to be Protestant Christians will do such things as that to carry the Catholic Church with them, it is not to be wondered at if they should be willing to resort to unconstitutional means to make their religious zeal effective in national law.

But when people professing to be Protestant Christians will do such things as that to carry with them the weight of the Catholic Church, is it not time they ceased to call themselves Protestants ? And when they will do such things *for any purpose*, is it not about time they should cease to call themselves Christians ? *Christianity* means *honesty*.

One more consideration just here: Is it consistent with either Protestant religious principles or American Constitutional principles to recognize the propriety of one man's absorbing into himself the personality of seven million two hundred thousand people, as they have granted to Cardinal Gibbons in this case?

By the evidences, logical, legal, Constitutional, and scriptural, which we have presented in this chapter, it is demonstrated that the Blair national Sunday bill is uncertain and unreasonable; that it is subversive of liberty, and savors of tyranny; and that it is unconstitutional and anti-Christian.

CHAPTER VI.

THE SUNDAY-LAW MOVEMENT IN THE FOURTH CENTURY, AND ITS PARALLEL IN THE NINETEENTH.

A TITLE for this chapter equally good with the above would be, The Making of the Papacy and the Perfect Likeness to It. In 2 Thess. 2 : 1–4, Paul wrote :—

"Now we beseech you, brethren, by the coming of our Lord Jesus Christ, and by our gathering together unto him, that ye be not soon shaken in mind, or be troubled, neither by spirit, nor by word, nor by letter as from us, as that the day of Christ is at hand. Let no man deceive you by any means ; for that day shall not come, except there come a falling away first, and that man of sin be revealed, the son of perdition ; who opposeth and exalteth himself above all that is called God, or that is worshiped ; so that he as God sitteth in the temple of God, showing himself that he is God ; for the mystery of iniquity doth already work."

Speaking to the elders of the church at Ephesus, Paul makes known what is the secret, we might say, the *spring*, of the papacy. Acts 20 : 28–30. "Of your own selves shall men arise, speaking perverse things, to draw away disciples after them." He was here speaking to the elders of the churches — the bishops. Whether he meant that there would be among these Ephesian bishops individuals who would do this, or that the bishopric would be perverted from its true office, and would exalt itself to the full development of the papacy, it matters not ; for the words themselves express the fact as it was enacted

(78)

in the history that followed. The bishopric of Rome finally developed into the papacy, which is the embodiment of the "mystery of iniquity." This work, as he says, began by the bishops' speaking perverse things, to draw away disciples after them. It became quite general about twenty years after the death of John. Says Mosheim : —

"The bishops augmented the number of religious rites in the Christian worship, by way of accommodation to the infirmities and prejudices both of Jews and heathen, in order to facilitate their conversion to Christianity." "For this purpose, they gave the name of *mysteries* to the institutions of the gospel, and decorated particularly the holy sacrament with that solemn title. They used in that sacred institution, as also in that of baptism, several of the terms employed in the heathen mysteries, and proceeded so far at length as to adopt some of the ceremonies of which those renowned mysteries consisted. This imitation began in the Eastern provinces ; but after the time of Hadrian [emperor A. D. 117–138], who first introduced the mysteries among the Latins, it was followed by the Christians who dwelt in the western part of the empire. A great part, therefore, of the service of the church in this century, had a certain air of the heathen mysteries, and resembled them considerably in many particulars." — *Church History*, cent. 2, part 2, chap. 4, par. 2, 5.

Another means by which these ambitious bishops secured disciples to themselves in great numbers from among the heathen, was the adoption of the day of the sun as a festival day.

"The oldest, the most wide-spread, and the most enduring of all the forms of idolatry known to man, [is] the worship of the sun."—*T. W. Chambers, in Old Testament Student*, January, 1886.

And says Mosheim : —

"Before the coming of Christ, all the Eastern nations performed divine worship with their faces turned to that

part of the heavens where the sun displays his rising
beams. This custom was founded upon a general opinion
that God, whose *essence* they looked upon to be *light*, and
whom they considered as being circumscribed within certain limits, dwelt in that part of the firmament from which
he sends forth the sun, the bright image of his benignity
and glory. The Christian converts, indeed, rejected this
gross error [of supposing that God dwelt in that part of
the firmament] ; but they retained the ancient and universal custom of worshiping toward the East, which sprang
from it. Nor is this custom abolished even in our times,
but still prevails in a great number of Christian churches."
Church History, cent. 2, part 2, chap. 4, par. 7. Eze. 8 : 16.

This was first adopted in connection with the Sabbath
of the Lord ; but after a while the paganized form of god-
liness crowded out the Sabbath entirely, and those were
cursed who would observe it. By the beginning of the
fourth century, this apostasy had gained a prominence by
which it could make itself felt in the political workings of
the Roman empire. The ambitious bishops of the apostasy
had at this time invented a theory of government, which
they determined to have recognized, which should make
the civil power subordinate to the ecclesiastical. Says
Neander : —

"There had in fact arisen in the church a false theocratical theory, originating not in the essence of the
gospel, but in the confusion of the religious constitutions
of the Old and New Testaments, which . . . brought
along with it an unchristian opposition of the spiritual to
the secular power, and which might easily result in the
formation of a sacerdotal State, subordinating the secular
to itself in a false and outward way." — *Torrey's Neander*,
Boston, 1852, p. 132.

The government of Israel was a true theocracy. That
was really a government of God. At the burning bush,
God commissioned Moses to lead his people out of Egypt.
By signs and wonders and mighty miracles multiplied,

God delivered Israel from Egypt, and led them through the wilderness, and finally into the promised land. There he ruled them by judges "until Samuel the prophet," to whom, when he was a child, God spoke and by whom he made known his will. In the days of Samuel, the people asked that they might have a king. This was allowed, and God chose Saul, and Samuel anointed him king of Israel. Saul failed to do the will of God, and as he rejected the word of the Lord, the Lord rejected him from being king, and sent Samuel to anoint David king of Israel; and David's throne God established forevermore. When Solomon succeeded to the kingdom in the place of David his father, the record is: "Then Solomon sat on the throne of the Lord as king instead of David his father." 1 Chron. 29:23. David's throne was the throne of the Lord, and Solomon sat on the throne of the Lord as king over the earthly kingdom of God. The succession to the throne descended in David's line to Zedekiah, who was made subject to the king of Babylon, and who entered into a solemn covenant before God that he would loyally render allegiance to the king of Babylon. But Zedekiah broke his covenant; and then God said to him : —

"Thou profane, wicked prince of Israel, whose day is come, when iniquity shall have an end, thus saith the Lord God · Remove the diadem, and take off the crown; this shall not be the same; exalt him that is low, and abase him that is high. I will overturn, overturn, overturn it; and it shall be no more, until he come whose right it is; and I will give it him." Eze. 21 25-27 ; 17 : 1-21.

The kingdom was then subject to Babylon. When Babylon fell, and Medo-Persia succeeded, it was overturned the first time. When Medo-Persia fell, and was succeeded by Grecia, it was overturned the second time. When the Greek empire gave way to Rome, it was overturned the third time. And then says the word, "It shall

6

be no more, till he come whose right it is; and I will give
it him." Who is he whose right it is? — "Thou . . . shalt
call his name Jesus. He shall be great, and shall be called
the Son of the Highest; and the Lord God shall give unto
him the throne of his father David; and he shall reign
over the house of Jacob forever, and of his kingdom there
shall be no end." Luke 1:31–33. And while he was here
as "that prophet," a man of sorrows and acquainted with
grief, the night in which he was betrayed he himself
declared, "My kingdom is not of this world." Thus the
throne of the Lord has been removed from this world, and
will "be no more, until he come whose right it is," and
then it will be given him. And *that time* is the end of
this world, and the beginning of "the world to come."
Therefore while this world stands, a true theocracy can
never be in it again. Consequently, from the death of
Christ till the end of this world, every theory of an earthly
theocracy is a false theory; every pretension to it is a
false pretension; and wherever any such theory is proposed or advocated, whether in Rome in the fourth century, or anywhere else in any other century, it bears in
it all that the papacy is or that it ever pretended to be,
— it puts a man in the place of God.

These theocratical bishops made themselves and their
power a necessity to Constantine, who, in order to make
sure of their support, became a political convert to the
form of Christianity, and made it the recognized religion
of the empire. And says Neander further: —

"This theocratical theory was already the prevailing
one in the time of Constantine; and . . . the bishops voluntarily made themselves dependent on him by their disputes, and by their determination to make use of the power
of the State for the furtherance of their aims." — *Idem.*

In these two quotations from Neander the whole history
of the papacy is epitomized. All that the history of the

papacy is, is only the working out of this theory. For
the first step in the logic of a man-made theocracy, is a
pope ; the second step is the infallibility of that pope ;
and the third step is the Inquisition, to make his infallibility effective, as we will prove : —

First, a true theocracy being a government immediately
directed by God, a false theocracy is a government directed
by a man in the place of God. But a man governing in the
place of God is a pope. A man ruling the world in the
place of God, is all that the pope has ever claimed to be.

Second, a false theocracy being a professed government of God, he who sits at the head of it, sits there
as the representative of God. He represents the divine authority ; and when he speaks or acts officially,
his speech or act is that of God. But to make a man
thus the representative of God, is only to clothe human
passions with divine power and authority. And being
human, he is bound always to act unlike God; and being clothed with irresponsible power, he will sometimes
act like the Devil. Consequently, in order to make all his
actions consistent with his profession, he is compelled to
cover them all with the divine attributes, and make everything that he does in his official capacity the act of God.
This is precisely the logic and the profession of papal infallibility. It is not claimed that all the pope speaks is
infallible ; it is only what he speaks officially — what he
speaks from the throne. Under this theory, he sits upon
that throne as the head of the government of God in this
world. He sits there as the representative of God. And
when he speaks officially, when he speaks from the throne,
he speaks as the representative of God. Therefore, sitting
in the place of God, ruling from that place as the official
representative of God, that which he speaks from the throne
is the word of God, and must be infallible. This is the
inevitable logic of the false theocratical theory. And if it

is denied that the theory is false, there is logically no
escape from accepting the papal system. The claims of
the papacy are not in the least extravagant, if the theory
be correct.

Third, God is the moral governor. His government is
a moral one, whose code is the moral law. His government
and his law have to do with the thoughts, the intents, and
the secrets of men's hearts. This must be ever the government of God, and nothing short of it can be the government of God. The pope then being the head of what
pretends to be a government of God, and ruling there in
the place of God, his government must rule in the realm
of morals, and must take cognizance of the counsels of the
heart. But being a man, how could he discover what
were the thoughts of men's hearts, whether they were
good or evil, that he might pronounce judgment upon
them? — By long and careful experiment, and by intense
ingenuity, means were discovered by which the most
secret thoughts of men's hearts might be wrung from
them, and that was by the Inquisition.

But the Inquisition was only the inevitable logic of the
theocratical theory upon which the papacy was founded.
The history of the papacy is only the logic of the theocratical theory upon which the papacy was founded : First,
a pope ; then the infallibility of that pope ; then the
Inquisition, to make his infallible authority effective.
And that is the logic of any theocratical theory of earthly
government since Jesus Christ died.

This being their theory, and their determination being
"to make use of the power of the State for the furtherance
of their aims," the question arises, What means did they
employ to secure control of this power? *Answer.* — *The
means of Sunday laws.* They secured from Constantine
the following Sunday law : —

"THE EMPEROR CONSTANTINE TO HELPIDIUS.

"On the venerable day of the sun, let the magistrates and people living in towns, rest, and let all work-shops be closed. Nevertheless, in the country, those engaged in the cultivation of land may freely and lawfully work, because it often happens that another day is not so well fitted for sowing grain and planting vines ; lest by neglect of the best time, the bounty provided by Heaven should be lost. Given the seventh day of March, Crispus and Constantine being consuls, both for the second time." [A. D. 321.]

This was not the very first Sunday law that they secured ; the first one has not survived. But although the first one has not survived, the reason for it has. Sozomen says that it was "that the day might be devoted with less interruption to the purposes of devotion." And this statement of Sozomen's is indorsed by Neander ("Church History," vol. 2, p. 298). This reason given by Sozomen reveals the secret of the legislation ; it shows that it was in behalf of the church, and to please the church.

By reading the above edict, it is seen that they started out quite moderately. They did not stop all work ; only judges, towns-people, and mechanics were required to rest, while people in the country might freely and lawfully work. The emperor paraded his soldiers on Sunday, and required them to repeat in concert the following prayer :—

"Thee alone we acknowledge as the true God ; thee we acknowledge as Ruler ; thee we invoke for help ; from thee have we received the victory ; through thee have we conquered our enemies ; to thee are we indebted for our present blessings ; from thee also we hope for future favors ; to thee we will direct our prayer. We beseech thee, that thou wouldst preserve our Emperor Constantine and his pious sons in health and prosperity through the longest life."

This Sunday law of A. D. 321 continued until 386, when —

"Those older changes effected by the Emperor Constantine were more rigorously enforced, and, in general, civil transactions of every kind on Sunday were strictly forbidden. Whoever transgressed was to be considered, in fact, as guilty of sacrilege." — *Neander, Id.*, p. 300.

Then as the people were not allowed to do any manner of work, they would play, and as the natural consequence, the circuses and the theaters throughout the empire were crowded every Sunday. But the object of the law, from the first one that was issued, was that the day might be used for the purposes of devotion, and the people might go to church. Consequently, that this object might be met, there was another step to take, and it was taken. At a church convention held at Carthage in 401, the bishops passed a resolution to send up a petition to the emperor, praying —

"That the public shows might be transferred from the Christian Sunday, and from feast days, to some other days of the week." — *Id.*

And the reason given in support of the petition was : —

"The people congregate more to the circus than to the church. And it is not fitting that Christians should gather at the spectacles, since the exercises there are contrary to the precepts of God ; and if they were not open, the Christians would attend more to things divine." — *Id.*, note 5.

That was all the trouble. Through the perverse doctrines, the ambitious schemes, and the worldly alliances of the bishops, the church had become filled with a mass of people, unconverted, who cared vastly more for worldly interests and pleasures than they did for religion. And as the government was now a government of God, it was

considered proper that the civil power should be used
to cause all to show respect for God, whether or not
they had any respect for him. But as long as they
could make something by working on Sunday, they
would work rather than go to church. A law was
secured forbidding all manner of Sunday work. Then
they would crowd the circuses and the theaters, instead
of going to church. But this was not what the bishops
wanted ; this was not that for which all work had been
forbidden. All work was forbidden in order that the
people might go to church ; but instead of that, they
crowded to the circus and the theater, and the audiences
of the bishops were rather slim. This was not at all
satisfying to their pride ; therefore the next step, and a
logical one, too, was, as the petition prayed, to have the
exhibitions of the circuses and the theaters transferred to
some other days of the week, so that the churches and the
theaters should not be open at the same time. For if
both were open, the Christians (?), as well as others, not
being able to go to both places at once, would go to the
circus or the theater instead of to the church. Neander
says : —

"Owing to the prevailing passion at that time, especially in the large cities, to run after the various public
shows, it so happened that when these spectacles fell on
the same days which had been consecrated by the church
to some religious festival, they proved a great hindrance
to the devotion of Christians, though chiefly, it must be
allowed, to those whose Christianity was the least an affair
of the life and of the heart." — *Id.*

Assuredly ! An open circus or theater will always
prove a great hindrance to the devotion of those Christians
whose Christianity is the least an affair of the life and of
the heart. In other words, an open circus or theater will
always be a great hindrance to the devotion of those who

have not religion enough to keep them from going to it, but who only want to use the profession of religion to maintain their popularity, and to promote their selfish interests. On the other hand, to the devotion of those whose Christianity is really an affair of the life and of the heart, an open circus or theater will never be a particle of hindrance, whether open at church time or all the time. But those people had not enough religion or love of right, to do what they thought to be right; therefore they wanted the State to take away from them all opportunity to do wrong, so that they could all be Christians. Satan himself could be made that kind of Christian in that way; but he would be Satan still.

Says Neander again : —

"Church teachers . . . were in truth often forced to complain that in such competitions the theater was vastly more frequented than the church." — *Id.*

And the church could not then stand competition ; she wanted a monopoly. And she got it.

This petition of the Carthage Convention could not be granted at once, but in 425 the desired law was secured ; and to this also there was attached the reason that was given for the first Sunday law that ever was made ; namely,—

"In order that the devotion of the faithful might be free from all disturbance."—*Id.*, p. 301.

It must constantly be borne in mind, however, that the only way in which "the devotion of the faithful" was "disturbed" by these things, was that when the circus or the theater was open at the same time that the church was open, the "faithful" would go to the circus or the theater instead of to church, and *therefore* their "devotion" was "disturbed." And of course the only way in which the "devotion" of such "faithful" ones could be freed from all disturbance, was to close the circuses and the theaters at church time.

In the logic of this theocratical scheme, there was one more step to be taken. It came about in this way : First the church had all work on Sunday forbidden, in order that the people might attend to things divine. But the people went to the circus and the theater instead of to church. Then the church had laws enacted closing the circuses and the theaters, in order that the people might attend to things divine. But even then the people would not be devoted, nor attend to things divine ; for they had no real religion. The next step to be taken, therefore, in the logic of the situation, was to compel them to be devoted — to compel them to attend to things divine. This was the next step logically to be taken, and it was taken. The theocratical bishops were equal to the occasion. They were ready with a theory that exactly met the demands of the case ; and the great Catholic Church Father and Catholic saint, Augustine, was the father of this Catholic saintly theory. He wrote : —

"It is indeed better that men should be brought to serve God by instruction than by fear of punishment, or by pain. But because the former means are better, the latter must not therefore be neglected. . . . Many must often be brought back to their Lord, like wicked servants, by the rod of temporal suffering, before they attain to the highest grade of religious development."— *Schaff's Church History*, vol. 2, sec. 27.

Of this theory Neander remarks : —

"It was by Augustine, then, that a theory was proposed and founded, which . . . contained the germ of that whole system of spiritual despotism of intolerance and persecution, which ended in the tribunals of the Inquisition."— *Church History*, p. 217.

The history of the Inquisition is only the history of

the carrying out of this infamous theory of Augustine's. But this theory is only the logical sequence of the theory upon which the whole series of Sunday laws was founded.

Then says Neander : —

"In this way the church received help from the State for the furtherance of her ends."

This statement is correct. Constantine did many things to favor the bishops. He gave them money and political preference. He made their decisions in disputed cases final, as the decision of Jesus Christ. But in nothing that he did for them did he give them power over those who did not belong to the church, to compel them to act as though they did, except in that one thing of the Sunday law. Their decisions, which he decreed to be final, were binding only on those who voluntarily chose that tribunal, and affected none others. Before this time, if any who had repaired to the tribunal of the bishops were dissatisfied with the decision, they could appeal to the civil magistrate. This edict cut off that source of appeal, yet affected none but those who voluntarily chose the arbitration of the bishops. But in the Sunday law, power was given to the church to compel those who did not belong to the church, and who were not subject to the jurisdiction of the church, to obey the commands of the church. In the Sunday law there was given to the church control of the civil power, that by it she could compel those who did not belong to the church to act as if they did. The history of Constantine's time may be searched through and through, and it will be found that in nothing did he give to the church any such power, except in this one thing — the Sunday law. Neander's statement is literally correct, that it was "in this way the church received help from the State for the furtherance of her ends."

Here let us bring together more closely the direct bearing of these statements from Neander. First, he says of the carrying into effect of the theocratical theory of those bishops, that they made themselves dependent upon Constantine by their disputes, and "by their determination to use the power of the State for the furtherance of their aims." Then he mentions the first and second Sunday laws of Constantine, the Sunday law of 386, the Carthage Convention, resolution, and petition of 401, and the law of 425 in response to this petition; and then, without a break, and with direct reference to these Sunday laws, he says: "*In this way* the church received help from the State for the furtherance of her ends." She started out with the determination to do it; she did it; and "*in this way*" she did it. And when she had secured control of the power of the State, she used it for the furtherance of her own aims, and that in her own despotic way, as announced in the Inquisitorial theory of Augustine. The first step logically and inevitably led to the last; and the theocratical leaders in the movement had the cruel courage to follow the first step unto the last, as framed in the words of Augustine, and illustrated in the history of the Inquisition.

LOOK ON THAT PICTURE, THEN ON THIS.

In a preceding chapter, we have given *verbatim* the Blair National Sunday bill, and have discussed some of its provisions. As we have seen, its object is clearly declared to be, to secure to the whole people rest on the Lord's day, and "to promote its observance as a day of worship;" and everything in the bill is to be construed, as far as possible, to secure the observance of the Sabbath "as a day of worship." This is the purpose of the bill: what is the purpose of those who are working so strenuously to have the bill become a law?

On Nov. 8, 1887, a convention was held in Elgin, Ill., which was "called by the members of the Elgin Association of Congregational Ministers and Churches, to consider the prevalent desecration of the Sabbath, and its remedy." In that convention, Dr. W. W. Everts, of Chicago, said : —

"This day is set apart for divine worship and preparation for another life. It is the test of all religion."

This clearly shows that the object of those who are working for Sunday laws is wholly religious, and that they are endeavoring to secure the power of the State to further their own aims. The Sabbath is indeed set apart for divine worship and preparation for another life ; but the observances of divine worship, and the preparation of men for another life, are committed by Jesus Christ to the church. The State cannot of right have anything to do with religious observances, and it is impossible for the civil power to prepare men for another life. Therefore, as this work belongs wholly to the church, and as the church wants to use the civil power for this purpose, it follows that these church leaders of our day, like those of the fourth century, are determined to make use of the power of the State to further their own aims.

"It is the test of all religion," says Dr. Everts. Then what can ever be the enforcement of it but the enforcement of a religious test? That is precisely what it is. Again, the same speaker said : —

"The people who do not keep the Sabbath, have no religion."

Very good. The antithesis of this is also true : the people who do keep the Sabbath have religion. Therefore this demand for laws to compel men to keep the Sabbath, is only a demand for laws to compel people to have religion

Again Dr. Everts said : —

" He who does not keep the Sabbath, does not worship God ; and he who does not worship God, is lost."

Admitted. Therefore this demand for laws to compel men to keep the Sabbath, is only a demand for laws to compel them to worship God.

Nor is Mr. Everts alone in this. Joseph Cook, in the Boston Monday lectureship of 1887, said : —

" The experience of centuries shows that you will in vain endeavor to preserve Sunday as a day of rest, unless you preserve it *as a day of worship*."

And Dr. Wilbur F. Crafts, in the Washington, D. C., national Sunday convention, Dec. 11–13, 1888, said : —

" If you take *religion* out of the day, you take the *rest* out of it."

These statements from the representative men of this movement, are sufficient to show that the movement is wholly religious. But, we repeat, religious observances and the promotion of religion, God has committed to the church only. Therefore this Sunday-law movement, as that in the fourth century, is only an effort on the part of the church to make use of the power of the State for the furtherance of her aims. More than this, to the church, and to her alone, God has committed the power by which alone religion can be promoted ; that is, the power of the Holy Spirit. So long as she has this power, she needs no other, and she will ask for no other. Therefore by this so widely prevalent movement on the part of the church to secure the power of the State by which to promote religion and religious observances, it is proved that the church is losing the power of the Holy Spirit.

The object of this movement is not only identical with that of the fourth century, but the arguments and methods used to attain that object are identical with those of the fourth century. There it was pleaded that without a Sunday law the people would not sufficiently attend to things divine.

At the Elgin convention, the following resolutions were passed : —

"*Resolved*, That we recognize the Sabbath as an institution of God, revealed in nature and the Bible, and of perpetual obligation on all men ; and also as a civil and American institution, bound up in vital and historical connection with the origin and foundation of our Government, the growth of our polity, and necessary to be maintained in order for the preservation and integrity of our national system, and therefore as having a sacred claim on all patriotic American citizens."

Let us read the commandment according to this resolution : Remember the Sabbath day, to keep it civilly The seventh day is the American Sabbath, and you shall keep it civilly, because in six days the Americans made the heavens and the earth, and on the seventh day they rested. Wherefore they blessed the Sabbath day, and civilized it.

"The seventh day is the Sabbath of *the Lord thy God*," is what the commandment says, and that is whose it is. The word *Sabbath* means rest. But the rest belongs to the one who rested. Who rested ? — God. From what ? — From the work of creation. "Remember the Sabbath day, to keep it holy," says the commandment. It is religious entirely. There is nothing either American or civil about it. It is the Lord's, and it is holy. If it is not kept holy, it is not kept at all. And being the Sabbath of the Lord — the Lord's day — it is to be rendered to the Lord, and not to Cæsar. With its observance or non-observance, civil government can never of right have anything to do. The second resolution was this : —

"*Resolved*, That we look with shame and sorrow on the non-observance of the Sabbath by many Christian people, in that the custom prevails with them of purchasing Sabbath newspapers, engaging in and patronizing Sabbath business and travel, and in many instances giving themselves to pleasure and self-indulgence, setting aside by neglect and indifference the great duties and privileges which God's day brings them."

That is a fact. They ought to be ashamed of it. But what do they do to rectify the matter? Do they resolve to preach the gospel better? to be more faithful themselves in bringing up the consciences of the people, by showing them their duty in regard to these things?—Oh, no. They resolve to do this:—

"*Resolved*, That we give our votes and support to those candidates or political officers who will pledge themselves to vote for the enactment and enforcing of statutes in favor of the civil Sabbath."

Yes, they are ashamed and sorry that Christians will not act like Christians, morally and religiously; therefore they will compel them to act both morally and religiously, by enforcing upon them a *civil* Sabbath! But if men will not obey the commandment of God, without being compelled to do it by the civil law, then when they obey the civil law, are they obeying God?— They are not. Do not these people, then, in that, put the civil law in the place of the law of God, and the civil government in the place of God?— They assuredly do. And that is always the inevitable effect of such attempts as this. It makes utter confusion of all civil and religious relations, and only adds hypocrisy to guilt, and increases unto more ungodliness. There is another important consideration just here. They never intend to secure nor to enforce a civil Sunday, but a religious one wholly; for in all the discussions of that whole convention, there was not a word said about a *civil*

Sabbath, except in two of these resolutions. In the discussions of the resolutions themselves, everything was upon a religious basis. There is no such thing as a civil Sunday; and no man can argue three minutes in favor of a civil Sunday, without making it only what it is, religious wholly.

In a Sunday-law mass-meeting held in Hamilton Hall, Oakland, Cal., in January, 1887, Rev. Dr. Briggs, of Napa, Cal., said to the State : —

"You relegate moral instruction to the church, and then let all go as they please on Sunday, so that we cannot get at them."

And so they want the State to *corral* all the people on Sunday, that the preachers may get at them. That is what they wanted in the fourth century. They got it at last.

They demand that the Sunday paper shall be abolished, because, as stated by Dr. Everts in the Elgin convention : —

"The laboring class are apt to rise late on Sunday morning, read the Sunday papers, and allow the *hour of worship* to go by unheeded."

And Dr. Herrick Johnson, in the Illinois Sunday convention, in Farwell Hall, Chicago, Nov 20, 21, 1888, said of the Sunday newspaper : —

"The saloon cannot come into our homes; the house of ill-fame cannot come into our parlors; but the Sunday paper is everywhere. It creeps into our homes on Sunday. It can so easily be put into the pocket and taken into the parlor and read."

Then he named the matter with which he said the Sunday papers are filled, — "crime, scandal, gossip, news, and politics," — and said : —

"What a *melange!* what a dish to set down before a man before breakfast and after breakfast, *to prepare him for hearing the word of God!* It makes it twice as hard to reach those who go to the sanctuary, and it *keeps man away from the house of worship altogether.* They read the paper; the time comes to go to church; but it is said, 'Here is something interesting; I will read it, and not go to church to-day.'"

The Sunday railway train must also be stopped, and for the same reason. In the speech above referred to, Dr. Johnson, speaking of the *Inter Ocean* Sunday news-train, described how the people would flock to the station to see the train, and said : —

"In the Sabbath lull from politics, business, etc., the people would go to church were it not for the attraction of the *Inter Ocean* special train."

In the Elgin convention, Dr. Everts said : —

"The Sunday train is another great evil. They cannot afford to run a train unless they get a great many passengers, and *so break up a great many congregations.* The Sunday railroad trains are hurrying their passengers fast on to perdition. What an outrage that the railroad, that great civilizer, should destroy the Christian Sabbath!"

And "Rev." M. A. Gault, of the National Reform Association, in the *Christian Statesman,* Sept. 25, 1884, said : —

"This railroad [the Chicago and Rock Island] has been running excursion trains from Des Moines to Colfax Springs on the Sabbath for some time, and the ministers complain that their members go on these excursions."

It is not necessary to add any more statements; they are all in the same line. They all plainly show that the secret and real object of the whole Sunday-law movement is to get the people to go to church. The Sunday train must be stopped, because church-members ride on it,

7

and don't go to church enough. The Sunday paper must be abolished, because the people read it instead of going to church, and because those who read it and go to church too, are not so well prepared to receive the preaching.

It was precisely the same way in the fourth century concerning the Sunday circus and theater. The people, even the church-members, would go to these instead of to church; and even if any went to both, it must be confessed that the Roman circus or theater was not a very excellent dish — "What a *melange!*" — to set down before a man to prepare him for hearing the word of God. The Sunday circus and theater could not afford to keep open unless they could get a great many spectators, and so break up a great many congregations. And as they hurried the spectators fast on to perdition, they had to be shut on Sunday, so as to keep "a great many congregations" out of perdition. It is exceedingly difficult to see how a Sunday circus in the fourth century could hurry to perdition any one who did not attend it; or how a Sunday train in the nineteenth century can hurry to perdition any one who does not ride on it. And if any are hurried to perdition by this means, who is to blame: the Sunday train, or the ones who ride on it? And Dr. Johnson's complaint of the Sunday papers' being worse than the saloon or the house of ill-fame, because these cannot get into the home, while the paper can be put into the pocket and taken into the home, is of the same flimsy piece. The saloon can be taken into the home, if a person will but put it into his pocket, and the house of ill-fame can be taken into the parlor, if a man will put it under his cloak; and if the Sunday paper gets there by being put into the pocket, where lies the blame: upon the paper, or upon the one who puts it into his pocket? Right here lies the secret of the whole evil now, as it did

in the fourth century: they blame everybody and everything else, even to inanimate things, for the irreligion,
the infidelity, and the sin that lie in their own hearts.

Nor are they going to be content with a little. Dr.
Crafts, speaking before the United States Senate committee in April, 1888, in favor of the National Sunday law,
said :—

"The law allows the local postmaster, if he chooses
(and some of them do choose), to open the mails at the
very hour of church, and so make the post-office the com-
petitor of the churches."

This same trouble was experienced in the fourth century also, between the circus or the theater, and the
church. The church could not stand competition; she
would be content with nothing less than a monopoly, and
she got it, precisely as these church managers are trying
to get it. More than this, they want now, as they did
then, the government to secure them in the enjoyment of
a perpetual monopoly. At another point in the same
speech, Mr. Crafts referred to the proposed law as one for
"protecting the church services from post-office competition." And in explaining how this could be done, he
said : —

"A law forbidding the opening between ten and twelve,
would accomplish this, and would be better than nothing ;
but we want more"

How much more ?   He continues : —

"A law forbidding any handling of Sunday mail at
such hours as would interfere with church attendance on
the part of the employees, would be better than nothing ;
but we want more than this."

How much more ?   He continues : —

"Local option in deciding whether a local post-office
shall be open at all on Sunday, we should welcome as

better than nothing ; . . . *but we desire more than this.*"

How much more ?   Still he continues : —

' "A law forbidding all carrier delivery of mail on Sunday, would be better than nothing ; *but we want more than that.*"

Then he says : —

"What we ask is a law instructing the postmaster-general to make no further contracts which shall include the carrying of mails on the Sabbath, and to provide that hereafter no mail matter shall be collected or distributed on that day."

But when they shall have secured the help of the Government in carrying their monopolizing ambition thus far, will they be content?—Not at all.   Nothing short of a complete and perpetual monopoly will satisfy them.   This is proved by Dr. Mc Allister's words at Lakeside, Ohio, July, 1887, as follows : —

"Let a man be what he may, — Jew, seventh-day observer of some other denomination, or those who do not believe in the Christian Sabbath, — let the law apply to every one, that there shall be no public desecration of the first day of the week, the Christian Sabbath, the day of rest for the nation.   They may hold any other day of the week as sacred, and observe it ; but that day which is the one day in seven for the nation at large, let that not be publicly desecrated by any one, by officer in the Government, or by private citizen, high or low, rich or poor."

There is much being said of the grasping, grinding greed of monopolies of many kinds ; but of all monopolies on earth, the most grinding, the most greedy, the most oppressive, the most conscienceless, is a religious monopoly

When they shall have stopped all Sunday work, and all Sunday papers, and all Sunday trains, in order that the people may go to church and attend to things divine, suppose that then the people fail to go to church or attend to things divine: will the religio-political managers stop there? Having done all this that the people may be devoted, will they suffer their good intentions to be frustrated, or their good offices to be despised? Will not these now take the next logical step, the step that was taken in the fourth century, and *compel* men to attend to things divine? If not, why not? Having taken all the steps but this, will they not take this?— They will. Human nature is the same now as it was in the fourth century. Politics is the same now as it was then. And as for religious bigotry, it knows no centuries; it knows no such thing as progress or enlightenment; it is ever the same. And in its control of civil power, the cruel results are also ever the same.

This probability is made yet more certain by the fact that the theory which is the basis of all this legislation, is also identical with that of the religio-political element in the fourth century. A theocratical theory of government was the basis of the religious legislation in the fourth century; it is the same now. The Woman's Christian Temperance Union is the most active and influential body in the Sunday-law movement now. The great majority of the petitions for the Blair Sunday law, except that of their seven-million-two-hundred-thousand-times-multiplied Cardinal, have been secured by the W. C. T. U.; and for convenience' sake we shall here repeat some quotations already given, showing the theory and purpose which that organization has in view:—

"A true theocracy is yet to come, and the enthronement of Christ in law and law-makers; hence I pray devoutly as a Christian patriot, for the ballot in the hands of women, and rejoice that the National Woman's Christian Temperance Union has so long championed this cause."

"The Woman's Christian Temperance Union, local, State, national, and world-wide, has one vital, organic thought, one all-absorbing purpose, one undying enthusiasm, and that is that Christ shall be *this world's king;* — yea, verily, THIS WORLD'S KING in its realm of cause and effect, — king of its courts, its camps, its commerce, — king of its colleges and cloisters, — king of its customs and its constitutions. . . . The kingdom of Christ must enter the realm of law through the gate-way of politics. . . . We pray Heaven to give them [the old parties] no rest . . . until they shall . . . swear an oath of allegiance to Christ in politics, and march in one great army up to the polls to worship God." — *President's Annual Address in Convention*, Nashville, 1887.

We have before shown that the W. C. T. U. is allied with the National Reform Association, and that their object is declared to be, upon a theocratical theory, to turn this republic into a kingdom of God. In the Cincinnati National Reform convention, 1872, Prof. J. R. W Sloane, D. D., said : —

"Every government by equitable laws, is a government of God. A republic thus governed is of Him, through the people, and is as truly and really a theocracy as the commonwealth of Israel."

By the expression "government by equitable laws," Mr. Sloane and the National Reformers generally mean such a government as the National Reformers seek to have established. According to their theory, our Government as it is, is not a government by equitable laws, but is entirely founded upon infidel and atheistic ideas. Consequently they want the Constitution religiously amended, and framed upon their ideas ; then it will be a government by equitable laws, and will be as truly and really a theocracy as was the commonwealth of Israel.

The Sunday-law Association also holds much the same theory. In the Elgin Sunday-law convention, Dr. Mandeville, of Chicago, said : —

"The merchants of Tyre insisted upon selling goods near the temple on the Sabbath, and Nehemiah compelled.

the officers of the law to do their duty, and stop it.   So we can compel the officers of the law to do their duty."

Now Nehemiah was ruling there in a true theocracy, a government of God ; the law of God was the law of the land, and God's will was made known by the written word, and by the prophets.   Therefore if Dr. Mandeville's argument is of any force at all, it is so only upon the claim of the establishment of a theocracy.   With this idea the view of Dr. Crafts agrees precisely, and Dr. Crafts is general secretary for the National Sunday-law Union. He claims, as expressed in his own words, that —

"The preachers are the successors of the prophets." — *Christian Statesman*, July 5, 1888.

Now put these things together.   The government of Israel was a theocracy ; the will of God was made known to the ruler by prophets ; the ruler compelled the officers of the law to prevent the ungodly from selling goods on the Sabbath.   This government is to be made a theocracy ; the preachers are the successors of the prophets ; and they are to compel the officers of the law to prevent all selling of goods and all manner of work on Sunday. This shows conclusively that these preachers intend to take the supremacy into their hands, officially declare the will of God, and compel all men to conform to it.   And this deduction is made certain by the words of Prof. Blanchard, in the Elgin convention : —

"In this work we are undertaking for the Sabbath, we are the representatives of God."

And the chief of these representatives of God, will be but a pope again ; because when preachers control the civil power as the representatives of God, a pope is inevitable.

These quotations prove, to a demonstration, that the whole theory upon which this religio-political movement is based, is identical with that of the fourth century, which established the papacy. They show also that the means employed — Sunday laws — by which to gain control of the civil power to make the wicked theory effective, are identical with the means which were employed in the fourth century for the same purpose. The next question is, Will they carry the theory into effect as they did in the fourth century and onward? In other words, when they get the power to oppress, will they use the power? A sufficient answer to this would seem to be the simple inquiry, If they do not intend to use the power, then why are they making such strenuous efforts to get it? But we are not left to this inquiry for an answer to the question; we have some of their own words. We may first refer the reader again to the quotations from the National Reformers on pages 51–56. And these quotations apply with special force to the question of Sunday observance; for they declare that —

"The observance of the Sabbath [Sunday] is an acknowledgment of the sovereign rights of God over us."

Then when they secure the law, it will be a national acknowledgment of the sovereign rights of God; and for any one to refuse to keep Sunday, will be treason, as declared by one of their own preachers (Rev. W. M. Grier, of Due West, South Carolina) in the Philadelphia convention, 1888: —

"Every sin, secret or public, against God, is a sin against our country, and is high treason against the State." — *Christian Statesman,* August 9, 1888.

Every sin, whether "secret or public," being "high treason" against the State, the State must punish it, even secret sin. But how shall the State discover secret sins, except by an Inquisition? This again confirms the logic of the theocratical theory of earthly government — that the Inquisition is the inevitable consequence.

Then so far as the National Reformers are concerned, it is certain that they are ready to use the power which they are doing their best to secure.

In the Elgin convention, Dr. Mandeville said further on the subject of Sunday laws : —

"When the church of God awakes and does its duty on one side, and the State on the other, we shall have no further trouble in this matter."

Yes, we remember how it was before, when the church and the State were united. The gentle Albigenses in Southern France greatly disturbed the church. But the church was wide awake ; for Innocent III. was pope. Philip Augustus was king of France ; and the church awoke the State with the cry, "Up, most Christian king! up, and aid us in our work of vengeance!" And thus, with the energy of the pope on one side, and of Philip on the other, the soldiers of Philip marched down upon the Albigenses, and swept them from the earth. And as "the church did its duty on one side and the State on the other," there was no further trouble in that matter.

In September, 1888, a minister in Selma, Cal., preaching on the subject of Sunday temperance and Sunday prohibition, said : —

"We have laws to punish the man who steals our property ; but we have no law to prevent people from working on Sunday. It is right that the thief be punished ; but I have more sympathy for that man than I have for him that works on that day."

Let that man have control of the power to compel a man to keep Sunday, and he will punish the man who works on Sunday, just as he would a thief.

At a National Reform W. C. T. U. convention held at Lakeside, Ohio, in 1887, the following question was asked : —

"Will not the National Reform movement result in persecution against those who on some points believe differently from the majority, even as the recognition of the Christian religion by the Roman power resulted in grievous persecution against true Christians?"

Answer, by Dr. Mc Allister : —

"Now notice the fallacy here. The recognition of the Roman Catholic religion by the State, made that State a persecuting power. Why? — Because the Roman Catholic religion is a persecuting religion. If true Christianity is a persecuting religion, then the acknowledgment of our principles by the State will make the State a persecutor. But if the true Christian religion is a religion of liberty, a religion that regards the rights of all, then the acknowledgment of those principles by the State will make the State the guardian of all men, and the State will be no persecutor. True religion never persecutes."

There is indeed a fallacy here; but it is not in the question; it is in the answer. That which made the Roman State a persecuting power, says the Doctor, was its recognition of the Catholic religion, "which is a persecuting religion." But the Roman Catholic religion is not the only persecuting religion that has been in the world. Presbyterianism persecuted while John Calvin ruled in Geneva; it persecuted while the Covenanters ruled in Scotland; it persecuted while it held the power in England. Congregationalism persecuted while it had the power in New England. Episcopalianism persecuted in England and in Virginia. Every religion that has been allied with the civil power, or that has controlled the civil power, has been a persecuting religion; and such will always be the case. Mr. Mc Allister's implied statement is true, that "true Christianity never persecutes;" but it is true only because true Christianity never will allow itself to be allied in any way with the civil power, or to receive any support from it. The National Reform Association does propose to "enforce upon all, the laws of Christian morality ;" it proposes to have the Government adopt the National Reform religion, and then "lay its hand upon any religion that does not conform to it ;" and it asserts that the civil power has the right "to command the consciences of men." Now any such thing carried into effect as is here plainly proposed by that Association, can never be anything else than persecution. But Mr. Mc Allister affirms that the National Reform movement, if successful, would not lead to persecution, "because true religion never persecutes." The Doctor's argument amounts only to this : The National Reform religion is the true religion. True religion never persecutes. Therefore to compel men to conform to the true religion, — that is, the religion that controls the civil power, — is not· persecution.

In A. D. 556, Pope Pelagius called upon Narses to compel certain parties to obey the pope's command. Narses refused, on the ground that it would be persecution. The pope answered Narses's objection with this argument : —

"Be not alarmed at the idle talk of some, crying out against persecution, and reproaching the church, as if she delighted in cruelty, when she punishes evil with wholesome severities, or procures the salvation of souls. *He alone persecutes who forces to evil.* But to restrain men from doing evil, or to punish those who have done it, is not persecution, or cruelty, but love of mankind." — *Bower's History of the Popes*, Pelagius, A. D. 556.

Compare this with Dr. Mc Allister's answer, and find any difference, in principle, between them, who can. There is no difference. The argument is identical. It is the essential spirit of the papacy which is displayed in both, and in that of Pope Pelagius no more than in that of Dr. Mc Allister.

Another question, or rather statement, was this : —

"There is a law in the State of Arkansas enforcing Sunday observance upon the people, and the result has been that many good persons have not only been imprisoned, but have lost their property, and even their lives."

Answer, by Dr. Mc Allister : —

"It is better that a few should suffer, than that the whole nation should lose its Sabbath."

This argument is identical with that by which the Pharisees in Christ's day justified themselves in killing him. It was said : —

"It is expedient for us that one man should die for the people, and that the whole nation perish not." John 11 : 50.

And then says the record : — .

"Then from that day forth they took counsel together for to put him to death." Verse 53.

The argument used in support of the claim of *right to use* this power, is identical with that used by the papacy in inaugurating her persecutions ; the argument in justification of the *use* of the power, is identical with that by which the murderers of Jesus Christ justified themselves in accomplishing that wicked deed ; and if anybody thinks that these men in our day, proceeding upon the identical theory, in the identical way, and justifying their proceedings by arguments identical with those of the papacy and the murderous Pharisees, — if anybody thinks that these men will stop short of persecution, he has vastly more confidence in apostate humanity than we have.

Nor are we left wholly to logical deduction in this. Dec. 14, 1887, Rev. W. T. McConnell, of Youngstown, Ohio, published in the *Christian Nation* an open letter to the editor of the *American Sentinel*, in which he said : —

"You look for trouble in this land in the future, if these principles are applied. I think it will come to you, if you maintain your present position. The fool-hardy fellow who persists in standing on a railroad track, may well anticipate trouble when he hears the rumble of the coming train. If he shall read the signs of the times in the screaming whistle and flaming head-light, he may change his position and avoid the danger ; but if he won't be influenced by these, his most gloomy forebodings of trouble will be realized when the express strikes him. So you, neighbor, if, through prejudice or the enmity of unregenerate hearts, you have determined to oppose the progress of this nation in fulfilling its vocation as an instrument in the divine work of regenerating human society, may rightly expect trouble. It will be sure to come to you."

Certainly it will. That is the spirit of the wicked scheme from the first effort ever made to secure a Sunday law unto this last.

We need not multiply evidences further, to show that this whole religio-political Sunday-law movement of our day is of the same piece with that in the fourth century. The theory is the same ; the means and the arguments are the same in both ; and two things that are so precisely alike in the making, will be exactly alike when they are made. That in the fourth century made the papacy ; and this in the nineteenth century will make a living likeness of the papacy

How appropriate, therefore, it is that Cardinal Gibbons should indorse the national Sunday bill! How natural, indeed, that he should gladly add his name to the number of petitioners in support of the movement to secure legislation in the interests of the church! He knows just how his brethren in the fourth century worked the thing ; he knows what the outcome of the movement was then ; and he knows full well what the outcome of this movement will be now. He knows that the theory underlying this movement is identical with the theory which was the

basis of that ; he knows the methods of working are the
same now as they were then ; he knows that the means
employed now, to secure control of the civil power, are
identical with the means employed then ; and he knows
that the result must be the same. He knows that when
religion shall have been established as an essential element
in legislation in this government, the experience of fifteen
hundred eventful years, and " the ingenuity and patient
care " of fifty generations of statesmen, will not be lost in
the effort to make the papal power supreme over all here
and now, as was done there and then. And in carrying
out the instructions of Pope Leo XIII., that " all Catholics
should do all in their power to cause the constitutions of
States and legislation to be modeled upon the principles
of the true church," the Cardinal assuredly *is* glad to have
the opportunity to add his name to the more than six millions of Protestants who are set for the accomplishment
of the same task.

To those so-called Protestants who are so anxious to
make religion a subject of legislation, it now appears very
desirable; and it also appears a very pleasant thing to secure
the alliance of the papacy. But when they shall have ac-
complished the feat, and find themselves in the midst of a
continuous whirl of political strife and contention with the
papacy, not alone for supremacy, but for *existence*,—then
they will find it not nearly so desirable as it now appears
to their vision, blinded by the lust for illegitimate power.

And when they find themselves compelled to pay more
than they bargained to, they will have but themselves to
blame ; for when they make religion a subject of legislation, they therein confess that it is justly subject to the
rule of majorities. And then, if the Romish Church se-
cures the majority, and compels the Protestants to conform to Catholic forms and ordinances, the Protestants
cannot justly complain.

CHAPTER VII

THE WORKINGS OF A SUNDAY LAW.

WE have shown by the literature and the logic of this whole Sunday-law question, that if the movement should succeed, it would be but the establishment of a religious despotism in this country. We have shown by their own statements that the principles held by the National Reformers are essentially papal, and that in the carrying out of these principles, they deliberately make propositions that betray the spirit of the Inquisition. But we are not compelled to stop with the principles or the logic of the case. We have some facts which show that such is the only effect of the kind of Sunday laws these people demand, as embodied in the Blair Sunday bill.

In 1885, Arkansas had Sunday laws reading as follows : —

"SECTION 1883. Every person who shall on the Sabbath, or Sunday, be found laboring, or shall compel his apprentice or servant to labor or perform service other than customary household duties of daily necessity, comfort, or charity, on conviction thereof shall be fined one dollar for each separate offense.

"SEC. 1884. Every apprentice or servant compelled to labor on Sunday shall be deemed a separate offense of the master.

"SEC. 1885. The provision of this act shall not apply to steamboats and other vessels navigating the waters of the State, nor such manufacturing establishments as require to be kept in continual operation.

"SEC. 1886. Persons who are members of any religious society who observe as Sabbath any other day of the week than the Christian Sabbath, or Sunday, shall not be subject to the penalties of this act (the Sunday law), so that they observe one day in seven, agreeable to the faith and practice of their church or society."

In the session of the Arkansas Legislature of 1885, Section 1886 was repealed, by act of March 3. The object of those who secured the repeal of that section, was, as they said, to close the saloons. It was claimed that under cover of that section, certain Jews who kept saloons in Little Rock, had successfully defied the law against Sunday saloons, and that there was no way to secure the proper enforcement of the law without the repeal of that section. The legislators believed the statements made, and repealed the section as stated.

The history of the repeal, according to the journals of the Senate and the House of the Arkansas General Assembly, is as follows :—

The legislature convened Jan. 12, 1885. January 24, Senator Anderson introduced a bill—Senate bill number 70—entitled, "A Bill to Prevent Sabbath-breaking," which was read the first time. January 26, it was read the second time, and referred to the Committee on Judiciary. January 31, it was reported back by Mr. Hicks, chairman of the committee, with the recommendation that it should pass. February 3, it was read the third time, and put upon its passage, and was carried by a vote of twenty-two to four. Absent or not voting, six. It was then sent to the House, and was read for the first time there February 3. The rules were then suspended ; it was read a second time, and was referred to the Committee on Judiciary Some amendments were offered, which were also referred to the committee, with the bill. February 24, this committee made the following report :—

" MR. SPEAKER : Your Committee on Judiciary, to whom was referred the Senate bill No. 70, a bill to prevent Sabbath-breaking, beg leave to report that they have had the bill under consideration, and herewith return the same, with the recommendation that it be passed without amendment.   · THORNBURGH, *Chairman*."

February 27, the bill was read the third time in the House, put upon its passage, and was carried by a vote of sixty-three to twenty-six. Absent or not voting, six. The same day, the House notified the Senate that it had passed Senate bill No. 70. March 7, 1885, the act received the approval of the governor, Simon P. Hughes.

Bear in mind that the object of this movement was said to be to close the saloons on Sunday ; and what discussion there was on the bill in both the Senate and the House, shows that such was the object, so far as the legislators understood it. But when the act was secured, and was framed into a law, not a saloon was closed, nor was there an attempt made, any more than before, to close them. Not one of the saloon-keepers was prosecuted. And in Little Rock itself, during the session of the legislature of 1887, when the law was in full force, up to the time of the restoration of the exemption clause, the saloons kept their doors wide open, and conducted their business with no effort at concealment, the same as they had before the act was passed. But, so far as we have been able to learn by diligent investigation, from the day of its passage, the law was used for no other purpose than to punish peaceable citizens of the State who observed the seventh day as the Sabbath, and exercised their God-given right to work on Sunday.

FIRST CASE.

Eld. J. W. Scoles.

Eld. J. W. Scoles, a Seventh-day Adventist minister, had gone from Michigan to Arkansas in June, 1884, to assist Eld. D. A. Wellman in holding some meetings at Springdale, Washington Co. As the result of these meetings, quite a number of persons adopted the faith of that body, and practiced accordingly. In August, 1884, Eld. Wellman died, and Eld. Scoles continued the work in that place. In the winter of 1884–85, Eld. J. G. Wood went from Appleton City, Mo., to assist Eld. Scoles at Springdale. A church was organized in that place early in 1885, and the erection of a meeting-house was begun at once. In addition to his subscription to the enterprise, Eld. Scoles agreed to paint the house when it should be ready. Further than this, we have the words of Eld. Scoles himself. He says : —

"I volunteered to do the painting as my share of the work, in addition to my subscription. I worked away at the church at odd times, sometimes half a day and sometimes more, as I could spare the time. The last Sunday in April, 1885, in order to finish the work so I could be free to go out for the summer's labor with the tent, and expecting to go the next day twenty miles, I went over to the church, and finished up a small strip of painting on the south side of the house, clear out of sight of all public roads ; and here I quietly worked away for perhaps two hours, in which time I finished it, and then went home. It was for this offense that I was indicted."

At the fall term of the Circuit Court held at Fayetteville, Mr. J. A. Armstrong, of Springdale, was summoned before the Grand Jury. He was asked if he knew of any violations of the Sunday law. He said he did.

Grand Jury. — "Who are they?"

Armstrong. — "The 'Frisco Railroad is running trains every Sunday."

G. J. — " Do you know of any others."

A. — " Yes ; the hotels of this place are open, and do a full run of business on Sunday, as on other days."

G. J. — " Do you know of any others ? "

A. — " Yes, sir ; the drug-stores and barber-shops all keep open, and do business every Sunday."

G. J. — " Do you know of any others ? "

A. — " Yes ; the livery-stables do more business on Sunday than on any other day of the week."

After several repetitions of this same form of questions and answers, in much the same manner, in relation to other lines of business, this question was reached : —

G. J. — " Do you know of any Seventh-day Adventists who ever work on Sunday ? "

A. — " Yes, sir."

After getting from the witness the names of his brethren, indictments were found against five persons, all of whom were Seventh-day Adventists. Eld. Scoles was one of the five. The indictment read as follows : —

"State of Arkansas }
              vs.   } *Indictment.*
J. W. Scoles. }

" The Grand Jury of Washington County, in the name and by the authority of the State of Arkansas, accuse J. W. Scoles of the crime of Sabbath-breaking, committed as follows ; viz., the said J. W. Scoles, on Sunday, the 26th day of April, 1885, in the county and State aforesaid, did unlawfully perform labor other than customary household duties of daily comfort, necessity, or charity, against the peace and dignity of the State of Arkansas.

"J. P. Henderson, *Pros. Att'y.*"

Mr Scoles was convicted. An appeal was taken to the Supreme Court of the State. October 30, 1886, the judgment of the Circuit Court was affirmed by the Supreme Court. Almost a score of cases essentially the same as the case of Eld. Scoles, were held over in the different Circuit Courts of the State, awaiting the decision of the Supreme Court in his case. All these cases now came up for trial, of which we print the facts : —

SECOND CASE.

Allen Meeks, Star of the West, Ark.

Mr. Meeks had been a resident of Arkansas since 1856, with the exception of one year. He had held the office of Justice of the Peace for a number of years both before and after the war. When he became a Seventh-day Adventist, he refused to hold the office longer, because its duties conflicted with his observance of the Sabbath.

Mr. Meeks was indicted at the July term of the Circuit Court, 1885, for Sabbath-breaking. He was arrested in November, 1885, and held under bonds of $500 for his appearance in January. The offense for which he was indicted, was planting potatoes on Sunday — the third Sunday in March, 1885. The work was done near Mr. Meeks's own house, and not nearer than two and a half miles to any public road or any place of public worship.

On the day referred to, Mr. La Fever and his wife went to visit Mr. Meeks at his home, and found Mr. Meeks planting potatoes. Mr. Meeks quit his work, and spent the rest of the day visiting with Mr. La Fever. La Fever afterward reported Mr. Meeks to the Grand Jury; and as the consequence, Mr. Meeks was indicted as stated. The fourth Monday in January, Meeks appeared before Judge Herne. His case was laid over to await the decision of the Supreme Court in the Scoles case.

THIRD CASE.

Joe McCoy, Magnet Cove, Ark.

Mr. McCoy moved from Louisville, Ky., to Arkansas, in 1873. He served as constable seven years, and two terms as Justice of the Peace, in Hot Springs County. In 1884, he became a Seventh-day Adventist. At the August, 1885, term of the Circuit Court in Hot Springs County, he was indicted for Sabbath-breaking, on the voluntary evidence of a Mr. Thomas Garrett.   The particular offense with which he was charged, was plowing on Sunday.   The witness was a Mr. Weatherford, a member of the Methodist Church.   The work was done half a mile from any public road, and entirely away from any place of public worship.

Mr. Weatherford went into the field where Mr. Mc Coy was plowing, and spent several hours with him, walking around as he plowed.   He was summoned as a witness in the case, by the Grand Jury.   In September, 1885, Mr. Mc Coy was arrested, and held under bonds for his appearance.   When he appeared at the February term of Court, his case, with others, was laid over to await the decision of the Supreme Court.

Mr. Mc Coy owned a small farm and a team, and foreseeing, as he thought, that they would soon be consumed in paying fines and costs, he could not in duty to his family and in harmony with his conscientious convictions of right and duty, allow all his property to go in that way ; neither could he afford to lose a whole day every week.   He therefore decided to abandon his farm, leaving it to satisfy the demands of the law against him in this case, and leave that country, hoping by this means to save at least his team and personal property.   By the advice of Eld. Dan. T. Jones, and at his earnest request, Mr. Mc Coy returned to Hot Springs County at the time for his appearance, February, 1887, and confessed judgment under the indictment.   A portion of the cost was remitted, and the fine and a portion of the cost were paid by Eld. Jones, and Mr. Mc Coy was released.

Mr. Mc Coy said to Eld. Jones, with tears in his eyes, that while he was reckless and wicked, he was not molested ; but as soon as he turned and tried to live a religious life, he was indicted and fined for it.

FOURTH CASE.

J. L. Shockey, Malvern, Ark.

Mr. J. L. Shockey was a Seventh-day Adventist who moved from Ohio in 1884, and settled on a piece of railroad land six miles north of Malvern, the county seat of Hot Springs Co., Ark.

About the middle of April, 1885, Mr. Shockey was plowing in his field on Sunday, one and three quarters of a mile from any place of public worship, and entirely out of sight of any place of worship. He was observed by D. B. Sims and C. B. Fitzhugh. He was reported to the Grand Jury by Anthony Wallace, a member of the Baptist Church. Sims and Fitzhugh were summoned as witnesses by the Grand Jury. Mr. Sims was hunting stock when he saw Mr. Shockey at work on Sunday. The Grand Jury found a true bill. Mr. Shockey was arrested Sept. 14, 1885, and gave bond to the amount of $110 for his appearance at the February term of the Circuit Court in the Seventh Judicial District, held at Malvern.   On the 1st day of February, 1886, Mr. Shockey appeared before Judge J. B. Wood.   In the meantime, the Scoles case had been appealed to the Supreme Court ; and at the request of the judge, the prosecuting attorney consented to continue the case, to await the decision of the Supreme Court.

FIFTH CASE.

James M. Pool.

James M. Pool, a Seventh-day Adventist, was indicted for Sabbath-breaking, at the fall term of the Circuit Court held at Fayetteville, beginning the first Monday in September, 1885.

He waived his right to jury trial. The only witness in the case was J. W. Cooper. Cooper was a member of the Presbyterian Church, and professed sanctification. He went to Pool's house on Sunday morning, to buy some tobacco, and found Pool hoeing in his garden ; so testified before the court, Judge Pittman presiding. The judge sustained the indictment, pronounced Pool guilty, and fined him one dollar and costs, amounting to $30.90.

SIXTH CASE.

James A. Armstrong, Springdale, Ark.

Mr. J. A. Armstrong moved from Warren Co., Ind., to Springdale, Ark., in 1878. In September, 1884, he joined the Seventh-day Adventist church at Springdale. November, 1885, he was indicted by the Grand Jury for Sabbath-breaking. On the 13th of February, 1886, he was arrested by William Holcomb, deputy-sheriff for Washington County, and was held under bonds of $250 for his appearance at the May term of the Circuit Court. The particular offense upon which the charge of Sabbath-breaking was based, was for digging potatoes in his field on Sunday. Millard Courtney was the prosecuting witness. Mr. Armstrong had a contract for building the school-house at Springdale. Mr. Courtney, with a friend, went to Armstrong's house on Sunday, to negotiate a contract for putting the tin roof on the school-house. From the house they went into the field where Mr. Armstrong was digging potatoes. There the business was all talked over, and the contract was secured for putting on the tin roof. Then this same Courtney became the prosecuting witness against Mr. Armstrong for working on Sunday.

On the first Monday in May, Mr. Armstrong appeared before Judge Pittman, Circuit Judge of the Fourth Judicial District, at Fayetteville ; and, waiving his right to jury trial, submitted his case to the Court for decision. Judge Pittman sustained the indictment. Fine and costs, amounting to $26.50, were paid, and Mr. Armstrong was released.

SEVENTH CASE.

William L. Gentry.

Mr. Gentry had been a citizen of Arkansas since 1849. He had served as Justice of the Peace for eight years, and then refused to accept the office longer. He had served as Associate-Justice of the County Court for two years. He had been a Seventh-day Adventist since 1877,—a member of the Seventh-day Adventist church at Star of the West, Pike Co., Ark.

At the January term of the Circuit Court, in 1886, he was indicted by the Grand Jury for Sabbath-breaking, the particular offense being his plowing on his own farm, July 2, 1886. He was arrested by the deputy-sheriff, and held under $500 bonds for his appearance at the July term of the Circuit Court. On the fourth Monday in July, Mr. Gentry appeared before Judge Herne, of the Eighth Judicial District. At his request, his case was continued, to await the decision of the Supreme Court in the Scoles case. In the month of January, 1887, his case was called for trial, as the Supreme Court had sustained the decision of the Circuit Court in the Scoles case. Mr. Gentry confessed judgment, but did not have the money to pay the fine and costs. Judge Herne ordered the defendant kept in custody until the fine and costs were paid. Mr. Gentry, having the confidence of the sheriff, was allowed the freedom of the town. On the last day of Court, the sheriff notified him that unless the fine and costs were paid, he would hire him out. The laws of Arkansas provide that in cases where the parties fail to satisfy the demands of the law, they shall be put up by the sheriff, and sold to the highest bidder, the bids being for the amount of wages to be paid per day. They are then worked under the same rules and regulations as convicts in the penitentiaries. Mr. Gentry was sixty-five years old, and not wishing to submit to such barbarous treatment, paid two dollars, all the money he had, and gave his note for the remaining amount, $26.80.

EIGHTH CASE.

Ples. A. Pannell, Star of the West, *Ark.*

Mr. Pannell, a Seventh-day Adventist, was indicted by the Grand Jury in January, 1886, for Sabbath-breaking, the particular offense charged being his plowing in his field on Sunday. He was arrested, and held under bonds of $250 for his appearance. At his request, his case was laid over to await the decision of the Supreme Court in the Scoles case. At the January term, in 1887, that case having been decided adversely, he appeared, and confessed judgment. His fine and costs amounted to $28.80 ; and not being able to pay, he was kept in jail four days, and then informed that unless some satisfactory arrangements were made, he would be sold, and would have to work out his fine and costs at seventy-five cents a day, the law not allowing the sheriff in such cases to accept less than that amount. Mr. Pannell paid two dollars in money, gave his note for $26.80, and was released.

NINTH CASE.

J. L. James, Star of the West, *Ark.*

Mr. James, a Seventh-day Adventist, was indicted by the Grand Jury in January, 1886, for Sabbath-breaking. The particular offense was for doing carpenter work on Sunday. The indictment was founded on the testimony of Mr. Powers, a minister of the Missionary Baptist Church. Mr. James was working on a house for a widow, near the Hot Springs Railroad. The work was done without any expectation of receiving payment, and wholly as a charitable act for the poor widow, who was a member of the

Methodist Church. Mr. James worked in the rain to do
it, because the widow was about to be thrown out of the
house in which she lived, and had no place to shelter her-
self and family.   Powers, the informer, lived about six hundred yards from where the work was done, and on that
very Sunday had carried wood from within seven rods of
where Mr. James was at work, and chopped up the wood
in sight of Mr. James.

Mr. James was arrested, and gave the usual bond for
his appearance in Court. He appeared before Judge Wood
at the January term of the Circuit Court of 1886.   His
case, with others, was laid over to await the decision of the
Supreme Court in the Scoles case.   The first Monday in
February, 1887, his case was called for trial.   He confessed
judgment ; the regular fine and costs were assessed, and
were paid by Eld. Dan. T. Jones, as the agent of Mr.
James's brethren at large.

TENTH CASE.

Mr. Allen Meeks, the second time.

At the January term in 1886, Mr. Meeks was indicted
the second time. July 13, he was arrested on a bench
warrant in the hands of William La Fever. Meeks gave
bonds for his appearance at the July term of Court. The
offense was for fixing his wagon-brake on Sunday. He
was reported to the Grand Jury by Riley Warren. Warren had gone to Meeks's house on the Sunday referred
to in the indictment, to see Mr. Meeks about hiring a
teacher for their public school, for both of them were
members of the school board of their district. In the
course of their conversation, Mr. Meeks incidentally mentioned having mended his wagon-brake that morning
This was reported to the Grand Jury by Mr. Warren, and
the indictment followed.

At the July term, this, with other cases mentioned, was held over to await the decision of the Supreme Court in the Scoles case.

At the January term in 1887, Meeks's case was called. He confessed judgment; the usual fine and costs were assessed, paid by Meeks, and he was released.

ELEVENTH CASE.

John A. Meeks, Star of the West, Ark.

John A. Meeks, aged fourteen years, son of Edward L. Meeks, was indicted by the Grand Jury at the January term of the Circuit Court of 1886, for Sabbath-breaking. The offense was for shooting squirrels on Sunday. The place where the squirrels were shot was in a mountainous district entirely away from any public road, or any place of public worship. He was reported by a Mr. M. Reeves. The sons of Mr. Reeves were hauling wood with a team on that same Sunday, and were present with the Meeks boy in the woods, and scared the squirrels around the trees for the Meeks boy to shoot. When the sport was over, the Meeks boy divided the game with the Reeves boys.

Then the father of the Reeves boys reported the Meeks boy, and he was indicted. His case was held over to await the decision of the Supreme Court in the Scoles case. At the January term in 1887, the boy confessed judgment, and was fined $5, and $3 county tax was assessed, and the costs, amounting in all to $22. The fine was paid, and the boy released.

TWELFTH CASE.

John Neusch, Magnet Cove, Ark.

Mr. Neusch is a fruit-raiser. On Sunday, June 21, 1885, he was gathering early peaches which were over-ripe, and were in danger of spoiling. He was half a mile from any public road, and some distance from any place of public worship, and not in sight of either. The orchard was on the top of a mountain, and Mr. Neusch was not seen by any one except a brother and a Mr. Hudspeth. Mr. Hudspeth was with Mr. Neusch about one hour. He went to see him in behalf of a young man who had been working for him, and who, with others, had been caught stealing peaches from Mr. Neusch's orchard on the preceding Sunday. Mr. Hudspeth offered Mr. Neusch pay for the peaches, if he would not report the young man. Mr. Neusch both refused to accept the money, and promised to say nothing about the offense, on condition that it should not be repeated.

February, 1886, Mr. Neusch was indicted for this offense of working on Sunday, as related. Neusch, having been advised that there was most probably an indictment filed against him, went to the county clerk and made inquiry in regard to the matter. The clerk handed him a writ for his arrest, and Neusch took it to the sheriff, and gave bond for his appearance at Court. In August, his case was laid over to await the decision of the Supreme Court in the Scoles case. As soon as that decision had been rendered, Neusch went and confessed judgment, and paid the fine and costs, amounting to $25. Mr. Neusch was an observer of the seventh day.

THIRTEENTH CASE.

F. N. Elmore, Springdale, Ark.

Mr. F. N. Elmore was indicted at the March term of the Circuit Court of 1886, on the charge of Sabbath-breaking. The indictment charged him with violating the Sunday laws by working on Sunday, Nov. 1, 1885. Mr. Elmore was arrested in April, 1886, by Deputy-Sheriff Wm. Holcomb, and was held in $250 bail for his appearance in the May term of the Circuit Court. On the 4th of

May, Mr. Elmore appeared before Judge Pittman, and waiving his right to jury trial, submitted his case to the Court for decision. Millard Courtney was the only witness examined. He testified that he had seen Mr. Elmore digging potatoes on the day above referred to, on the premises of Mr. J. A. Armstrong. This work was done by Elmore on the day when Courtney took his friend to Armstrong to secure the contract for putting the tin roofing on the school-house ; and that is how Courtney knew Elmore had worked on that day. Elmore was convicted. The fine and costs were $28.95, which was paid, and he was released. Mr. Elmore was a Seventh-day Adventist.

FOURTEENTH CASE.

William H. Fritz, Hindsville, Madison Co., Ark.

Mr. Fritz was indicted at the April term of the Circuit Court in 1886, for Sabbath-breaking, and held under $250 bonds for his appearance at the September term, at Huntsville. Mr. Fritz is a wood-workman, and the offense charged was for working in the shop on Sunday. The shop was in the country, and two hundred yards from the public road. The indictment was sustained. The defendant was fined one dollar and costs, amounting to $28. Mr. Fritz was a Seventh-day Adventist.

FIFTEENTH CASE.

Z. Swearingen.

Mr. Z. Swearingen was a member of the church of Seventh-day Adventists. Went from Michigan to Arkansas in 1879, and settled on a small farm eleven miles south of Bentonville, the county seat of Benton County. He and his son Franz, aged seventeen years, were indicted by the Grand Jury at the April term of the Circuit Court of 1886, upon the charge of Sabbath-breaking by "performing labor other than customary household duties of daily comfort, necessity, or charity, against the peace and dignity of the State of Arkansas, on Feb. 14, 1885," the same day being Sunday.

Both were arrested by F. P. Galbraith, sheriff of Benton County, in May, 1886, and were put under bond of $250 for their appearance at the fall term of the Circuit Court. Sept. 27, 1886, the defendants appeared before Judge Pittman, of the Fourth Judicial District.

John G. Cowen, witness for the State, testified that he saw Mr. Swearingen and his son hauling rails on Sunday, the 14th day of February, 1885, as he returned from the funeral of Mrs. Boggett. Hon. J. W. Walker, attorney for the defendants, explained to the jury that the defendants conscientiously observed the seventh day of the week as the Sabbath, in accordance with the faith and practice of the church of which they were members. The prosecuting attorney stated to the jury that it was "one of those Advent cases." Jury found the defendants guilty, as charged in the indictment. As Mr. Swearingen did not have the money to pay the fine and costs for himself and son, amounting to $34.20, they were sent to jail until the money should be secured.

They were put in jail Oct. 1, 1886. On the 13th of the same month, the sheriff levied on, and took possession of, a horse belonging to Mr. Swearingen. The horse sold at sheriff's sale, the 25th of the same month, for $26.50, leaving a balance against Mr. Swearingen of $7.70; yet both he and his son were released the same day that the horse was sold. On the 15th day of December, the sheriff appeared again on the premises of Mr. Swearingen, and presented a bill for $28.95. Of this sum, $21.25 was for the board of Mr. Swearingen and son while in jail, and $7.70, balance on the fine. Mr. Swearingen had no money to pay the bill. The sheriff levied on his mare, har-

ness, wagon, and a cow and calf. Before the day of the
sale, however, Mr. Swearingen's brethren raised the money
by donations, paid the bill, and secured the release of his
property. One thing about this case is to be noted particularly : The witness upon whose testimony these people
were convicted, said that he saw them hauling rails on
Sunday, the 14th day of February, as he returned from
the funeral of Mrs. Boggett. Now, the act under which
this prosecution was carried on, became a law March 3,
and was approved by the Governor, March 7. Consequently, they were convicted for work done seventeen
days before the act was passed under which they were
convicted.

SIXTEENTH CASE.

I. L. Benson.

Mr. Benson was not at that time a member of any
church, made no pretensions to religious faith, and did not
observe any day. He had the contract for painting the
railroad bridge across the Arkansas River at Van Buren,
Ark. He worked a set of hands on the bridge all days of
the week, Sundays included. In May, 1886, Mr. Benson
and one of his men were arrested on the charge of
Sabbath-breaking. They were taken to Fort Smith, and
arraigned before a Justice of the Peace. The Justice did
not put them through any form of trial, nor even ask
them whether they were guilty or not guilty, but read a
section of the law to them, and told them he would make
the fine as light as possible, amounting, with costs, to
$4.75 each. They refused to pay the fines, and were
placed in custody of the sheriff. The sheriff gave them
the freedom of the place, only requiring them to appear
at the Justice's office at a certain hour. Mr. Benson
telegraphed to the general manager of the railroad in
regard to the matter. The general manager telegraphed
to his attorney in that city, to attend to the cases.

Mr. Benson and his men appeared before the Justice for a hearing in their cases. It was granted, with some reluctance. The attorney, Mr. Bryolair, told the Justice it was a shame to arrest men for working on the bridge at the risk of their lives to support their families, when the public work in their own town was principally done on Sunday. A hearing was granted, and the trial set for the next day.

They were not placed under any bonds at all, but were allowed to go on their own recognizance. The following day, a jury was impaneled and the trial begun. The deputy-sheriff was the leading witness, and swore positively that he saw them at work on Sunday. The jury brought in a verdict to the effect that they had "*agreed to disagree.*" This was on Wednesday. The following Monday was set for a new trial. No bond was even at this time required. The defendants appeared at the time appointed, and plead not guilty. The Justice, after giving them a brief lecture, dismissed the case.

Since that time Mr. Benson has become a Seventh-day Adventist, and perhaps would not have fared so easily had he been a Seventh-day Adventist when he was indicted.

SEVENTEENTH CASE.

James A. Armstrong, the second time.

On the 9th of July, 1886, Mr. Armstrong was arrested the second time, by A. M. Dritt, marshal of Springdale, for working on Sunday, June 27, and taken before the mayor, S. L. Staples. When brought before the mayor, Mr. Armstrong called for the affidavit on which the writ was issued. The mayor stated that he himself had seen Mr. Armstrong at work in his garden on Sunday, and that Mr. A. J. Vaughn had called his attention to Armstrong while he was at work, and had said : "Now, see that you do your duty." This made an affidavit unnecessary. The case was tried before the mayor, acting as Justice of the Peace. A. J. Vaughn was the first witness.

Justice of the Peace. — "What do you know about Mr. Armstrong's working on Sunday, June 27?"

Vaughn. — "I did not see Armstrong at all that day ; I only heard he was at work."

J. I. Gladden was the next witness called.

Justice. — "What do you know about Mr. Armstrong's working on Sunday, June 27?"

Gladden. — "While at the depot, I saw some one at work hoeing in Mr. Armstrong's garden ; but I do not know for certain who it was."

Millard Courtney was the next witness called.

Justice. — "Tell us what you know about Mr. Armstrong's working on the Sunday in question."

Courtney. — "While on the platform of the depot, I saw some one hoeing in Mr. Armstrong's garden. I am not positive who it was."

Having failed to prove anything from the witnesses regularly summoned, the case was "rested" while the marshal was sent out to find somebody else. He brought in Gideon Bowman, who was then questioned as follows :—

Justice. — "Do you know anything about Mr. Armstrong's doing work other than customary household duties of daily necessity, comfort, or charity on the Christian Sabbath, June 27?"

Bowman. — "I do."

J. — "State what you saw."

B. — "As I came into town, having been out east, in passing Mr. Armstrong's house, I saw him hoeing in the garden."

J. — "Did you recognize this person to be J. A. Armstrong?"

B. — "I did."

9

Here the prosecution rested the case, and Eld. J. G. Wood assumed the cross-examination in behalf of the prisoner.

Wood. — " Mr. Bowman, you say you were coming along the road from the east when you saw Mr. Armstrong at work in his garden ? "

B. — " I did."

W. — " Were you coming to town ? "

B. — " I was."

W. — " About how long were you in passing Mr. Armstrong's house ? and what was the length of time you saw him at work ? "

B. — " I can't tell."

W. — " Do you think the time to have been two minutes, or more ? "

B. — " Don't know ; can't tell."

W. — " Could it possibly have exceeded one minute ? "

B. — " I don't know. It makes no difference. I am not here to be pumped."

W. — " Mr Bowman, we are only wanting the facts in the case. Are you sure it was Mr. Armstrong you saw hoeing ? Might it not have been some other man ? "

B. — " I am not mistaken. I know it was J. A. Armstrong."

W. — " What was he doing ? "

B. — " I told you he was hoeing."

W. — " What was he hoeing ? Was he hoeing corn, or hoeing out some potatoes for his dinner ? "

B. — " He was hoeing ; that is enough."

At this point the Justice of the Peace interfered : —

" It seems, Mr. Wood, that you are trying to make it appear that Mr. Armstrong was only digging a mess of potatoes for his dinner. If that is so, and he was doing a work of comfort, necessity, or charity, he can prove it."

W. — " If your honor please, Mr. Armstrong is not here to prove a negative. The law allows him to do such work as is of necessity, comfort, or charity ; and until it is clearly proven that he has violated this law, which thus far has not been proven, it is unnecessary for him to offer proof. A man stands innocent until he is proven guilty "

Justice. — "We proceed."

W. — "Mr. Bowman, you say you were in the road when you saw Mr. Armstrong?"

B. — "Yes."

W. — "Do you remember whether there was a fence between you and Mr. Armstrong?"

B. — "Yes ; there was."

W. — "About what is the hight of that fence?"

B. — "Do n't know."

W. — "Was it a board fence five boards high?"

B. — "Can't say."

W. — "Was there a second fence between the road and the garden, beyond the house and lot?"

B. — "I think there was."

W. — "Was that second fence a board fence or a very high picket fence?"

B. — "I do n't know, nor do n't care. It makes no difference."

W. — "I understand, then, that you do n't know. Well, Mr. Bowman, what time in the day did you see Mr. Armstrong in the garden?"

B. — "In the afternoon."

W. — "About what time in the afternoon, — was it one or two o'clock, or later?"

B. — "It makes no difference. I am not here to be pumped. If you want to pump me any more, just come out on the street with me."

W. — "Sir, I have no desire to pump anything but truth from you, and only wish to know the facts in this case. Was it about one or two o'clock in the afternoon, or about four or five? Please tell us about the time of day."

B. — "It was between twelve noon and sunset. That is near enough."

This closed the testimony in the case. Mr. Armstrong was declared guilty, and fined one dollar and costs, the whole amounting to $4.65. In default of the payment of his fine, the mayor, acting as Justice of the Peace, told him he would send him to the county jail, and allow him a dollar a day until the fine and costs were paid.

The marshal went at once to the livery-stable to get a rig, and within four hours from the time of his arrest, Mr. Armstrong, in charge of the marshal, was on his way to jail at Fayetteville. He was locked up with another prisoner, with nothing but a little straw, and a dirty blanket about thirty inches wide, for a bed for both. The next night, he was allowed to lie in the corridor on the brick floor, with his alpaca coat for a bed, and his Bible for a pillow. The third night, a friend in town furnished him a quilt and a pillow. On the fourth night, his friend brought him another quilt, and thus he was made quite comfortable On the fifth day, at noon, he was released.

When Mr. Armstrong returned to Springdale, the mayor notified him that his fine and costs were not satisfied, and that unless they were paid in ten days, an execution would be issued, and his property sold. Mr. Armstrong filed an appeal to the Circuit Court, and the appeal was sustained, and he was released from further penalty.

EIGHTEENTH CASE.

J. L. Munson, Star of the West, Ark.

Mr. Munson, a Seventh-day Adventist, was indicted by the Grand Jury at the July term of the Circuit Court of 1886, for working on a Sunday in March, 1886. Mr. Munson was cutting briars out of his fence corner at the back of his field, one fourth of a mile from any public road, and one and one half miles from any place of public worship. He was indicted on the voluntary evidence of Jeff. O'Neal, a Free-will Baptist preacher. He was arrested Nov. 3, 1886, and held under bonds of $300 for his appearance January, 1887. He confessed judgment, and Judge Herne assessed the legal fine of one dollar, with three dollars county tax, and costs, amounting to $14.20. This was paid by Mr. Munson, and he was released.

NINETEENTH CASE.

James M. Pool, the second time.

Mr. Pool was indicted the second time at the September term of Court in 1886, and was held under bonds of $250 for his appearance May 16, 1887. The act under which these prosecutions were conducted, was repealed before the date of trial. Pool was tried under the indictment, and fined one dollar and costs, amounting to $28.40.

TWENTIETH CASE.

J. L. Shockey, the second time

In August, 1886, Mr. P. Hammond, a member of the Baptist Church, appeared before the Grand Jury in Hot Springs County, and charged J. L. Shockey with hauling rails and clearing land on Sunday, the first day of the week, July 11, 1886. The Grand Jury presented an indictment. On Dec. 14, 1886, Mr. Shockey was arrested and taken to Malvern, locked up until the next day, when he gave the usual bond for his appearance at Court, and was released. The work for which Mr. Shockey was indicted, was done on a new farm which he was opening up in the woods, three fourths of a mile from any public road, and more than a mile from any place of public worship, and not in sight of either. The witness, Mr. Hammond, passed by where Mr. Shockey was at work, and after he had gone some distance, returned, and spoke to Mr Shockey about buying from him a Plymouth Rock rooster. The bargain was then made, Hammond agreeing to pay Shockey fifty cents for the rooster.

Shockey was indicted, and his case set for trial Feb. 7, 1887. This case, with the one before mentioned and some others that had been held over to await the decision in the Scoles case, was called, and February 11 fixed as the day of trial for all.

In the meantime, Eld. Dan. T. Jones, president of the Missouri Conference of Seventh-day Adventists, had an interview with the prosecuting attorney, Mr. J. P. Henderson, and explained the nature of all these cases, and showed him that the Adventists were faithful, law-abiding citizens in every respect, except in this matter of working on Sunday; that the defendants in the cases were all poor men, some of whom were utterly unable to pay any fines and costs, and consequently would have to go to jail; and asked Mr. Henderson if he would be willing to remit a portion of his fees, which were ten dollars in each case, provided the remainder was raised by donations by the Seventh-day Adventists throughout the country, for the relief of their brethren in Arkansas.

Mr. Henderson replied that if these cases were of the nature of religious persecution, he would not feel justified in taking any fees. He said he would not be a party to any such action, but would want some time to investigate the cases, to satisfy himself that this was true. Upon investigation, he became fully satisfied that the prosecutions were simply of the nature of religious persecutions, and generously refused to take any fees in any of the cases.

When the cases were called, the defendants confessed judgment, and the fine prescribed by law was assessed. The county clerk reduced his fees about one half; the sheriff, one half of his; and the prosecuting attorney, all of his, which reduced the total expenses about one half. The remainder was advanced from funds supplied by Seventh-day Adventists throughout the country, for the relief of their brethren in Arkansas.

TWENTY-FIRST CASE.

Alexander Holt, Magnet Cove, Ark.

Mr. Holt, a Seventh-day Adventist, was a medical student of the Memphis Hospital and Medical College, Memphis, Tenn.

In 1885 he was working on a farm in the northern part of Hot Spring Co., Ark. At the February term of the Circuit Court in 1886, he was indicted for Sabbath-breaking. The particular charge was working on Sunday, Oct. 11, 1885.

C. C. Kaufman was the informer. Mr. Holt had worked one Sunday near a public road, but not nearer than a mile to any place of public worship. Hearing that there had been an indictment found against him, Mr. Holt did not wait for the sheriff to come for his arrest, but went to the county seat, ten miles distant, taking a bondsman with him, and inquired of the proper officer if there was an indictment against him. The warrant for his arrest was then read to him by the deputy-sheriff. Holt gave bonds to appear at the August term of the Circuit Court, and was released.

At the August term of Court, the case was laid over to await the decision of the Supreme Court in the Scoles case. February, 1887, Holt's case was called for trial at Malvern. The Supreme Court having decided adversely, Holt confessed judgment, and paid the fine and costs, amounting to $28.

There were a number of other cases, but they are all of the same kind,—causeless arrests upon information treacherously obtained to vent religious spite.

In January, 1887, a bill was introduced by Senator R. H. Crockett, restoring the protective clause to observers of the seventh day. But two men voted against the bill in the Senate, and both these were preachers. One of them, a member from Pike County, was acquainted with many who observed the seventh day, several of whom were at that time under bonds. In private conversation, he confessed that they were all excellent people and law-abiding citizens. When the vote was taken by roll-call, he asked to explain his vote, and the following note of explanation was sent to the clerk :—

"MR. PRESIDENT: I desire to explain my vote. Believing as I do that the Christian Sabbath should be observed as a day of worship, losing sight of this is to impede the progress of Christianity.   J. P. COPELAND."

The vote was a verbal and emphatic "No."

The restoration of this protective section was strenuously opposed by the religious leaders. The editor of the *Arkansas Methodist* declared in his paper at the time, that "the Sabbath laws" as they were, without the protective section, had "worked well enough," and were "about as near perfect as we can expect to get them, under the present Constitution."

There are some points in these cases that deserve a word of comment: —

First, with two exceptions, all the arrests and prosecutions were of people who observed the seventh day of the week as the Sabbath. And in these two exceptions, those who were held for trial were held without bail, — simply on their own recognizance, — and the cases both dismissed; while in every case of a Seventh-day Adventist, the least bail that was accepted was $110; the most of them were held under bonds for $250, and some for as high as $500. There was not a single case dismissed, and in all the cases there never was a complaint made of that which was done having disturbed the worship or the rest of any one. But the indictments were all for the crime of "Sabbath-breaking" by the performance of labor on Sunday. If there had been arrests of other people for working on Sunday, in anything like the numbers that there were of seventh-day observers, and the law had been enforced upon all alike, then the iniquity would not have been so apparent; or if those who were not seventh-day observers, and who were arrested, had been convicted, even then the case would not have been so clearly one of persecution. But when in all the record of the whole two years' existence of the law in this form, there was not a solitary saloon-keeper arrested, there was not a person who did not observe the seventh day arrested, with the two exceptions named, then there could be no clearer demonstration that the law was used only as a means to vent religious spite against a class of citizens guiltless of any crime, but only of professing a religion different from that of the majority. Nothing could be more clearly demonstrated than is this: that the only effect of the repeal of that exemption clause was to give power to a set of bigots to oppress those whose religion they hated. If anything was needed to make the demonstration more clear, it is found in the method of the prosecutions.

Mr. Swearingen was convicted upon the testimony of a witness who swore that the work for which he was convicted was done on a day which proved to be *seventeen days before the law was enacted*, thus by its enforcement making the law *ex post facto*. The Constitution of the United States forbids the making of *ex post facto* laws. But when a law not being *ex post facto* in itself, is made so by its enforcement, it is time that something was being done to enlighten courts and juries upon that subject, even though it should be by an amendment to the Constitution of the United States, providing that no law not being *ex post facto* in itself shall be made so by its enforcement. Then, on the other hand, several cases were tried and the men convicted and fined *after the law was repealed*, but for work done before.

Second, in almost every case the informer or the prosecuting witness, or perhaps both, was a man who was doing work or business on the same day, and sometimes with the very persons accused; yet the man who kept the seventh day was convicted in every instance, while the man who did not keep the seventh day, but did work or business with the man who was prosecuted, was

left entirely unmolested, and his evidence was accepted in
Court to convict the other man. For instance, Millard
Courtney, the one who was the prosecuting witness
against both Armstrong and Elmore, took a man with
him to where these men were working, and there made a
contract for roofing a school-house; and yet this man's
evidence convicted these two men of Sabbath-breaking at
the very time at which he was doing business with them.

Third, J. L. Shockey was convicted of Sabbath-breaking upon the testimony of Hammond, who went where he
was at work, and bought of him a Plymouth Rock rooster.

Fourth, J. L. James, who worked in the rain for nothing, that a poor widow might be sheltered, was convicted
of Sabbath-breaking upon the evidence of a man who carried wood and chopped it up within seven rods of the man
who was convicted by his testimony.

Fifth, La Fever and his wife went to Allen Meeks's
house on Sunday to visit. They found Meeks planting
potatoes. Meeks stopped planting potatoes, and spent
the rest of the day visiting with them; and yet Meeks
was convicted and fined upon the evidence of La Fever.

Sixth, the second case of this same Meeks. Riley
Warren went to his house on Sunday, to see him about
hiring a teacher for the public school. In the social,
neighborly conversation that passed between them, Meeks
incidentally mentioned that he had mended his wagon-
brake that morning; and yet he was convicted of Sabbath-breaking by the evidence of that same Riley Warren.
And further, Meeks was thus virtually compelled to be a
witness against himself,—clearly another violation of both
the State and the United States Constitution.

Seventh, Mr. Reeves's boys were hauling wood on Sunday. In the timber where they got the wood, they met
another boy, John A. Meeks, hunting squirrels. They
joined him in the hunt, scaring the squirrels around

the trees so he could **shoot them.** Then the squirrels were divided **between the Meeks boy and** the Reeves **boys.** Then the Meeks boy was **indicted,** prosecuted, and convicted **of** Sabbath-breaking upon **the** evidence **of the** father of **those** boys who were hauling wood, **and who** helped to **kill the** squirrels.

Eighth, **James M. Pool, for hoeing** in his garden **on Sunday, was** convicted of Sabbath-breaking, on **the evi** dence of a "sanctified" church-member who had gone **to** Pool's house on Sunday to buy tobacco.

Thus throughout this whole list of cases, people **who** were performing **honest labor** on their **own premises in a** way in which **it was impossible to do harm to any soul on** earth, **were indicted, prosecuted,** and **convicted** upon **the** evidence **of men who, if there** were **any wrong** involved in the **case at** all, **were more guilty than they.** If relig ious persecution **could possibly be more clearly** demon strated **than it is in this thing, we hope never to see** an illustration **of it.**

Yet further : **Take the** methods **of prosecution. In the** case of Scoles, J. A. Armstrong **was** called before **the** Grand Jury. After repeated **answers to** questions **in** regard to **Sunday** work by different parties **in several** different lines of **business** and traffic, **he was** asked the direct question whether he knew of any Seventh-day Ad ventists who worked **on** Sunday, and when **in the** nature of the case he **answered in** the affirmative, **every** one of the Seventh-day **Adventists** whom he named was indicted, and not one **of any other class** or trade. And in the second case of James A. **Armstrong ; although, when** asked for the **affidavit upon which Armstrong was** arrested, the mayor **said** that **A. J. Vaughn had called his** attention to Armstrong's **working, and** had said, **"Now** see that you do your **duty," yet Vaughn** testified **under** oath that **he** did **not see Armstrong at all on the day** referred to.

Armstrong was arrested at the instance of the mayor, and tried before the mayor, who acted as Justice of the Peace. This made the mayor, virtually, both prosecuting witness and judge ; and the questions which he asked show that that was precisely his position, and his own view of the case. The question which he asked to each of the first two witnesses was, "What do you know about Mr. Armstrong's working on Sunday, June 27?" This question assumes all that was expected to be proved on the trial. And then when the only witness whose word seemed to confirm the judge's view of the case, was cross-questioned, the judge came to the rescue with the excellent piece of legal wisdom, to the effect that if the prisoner was innocent, he could prove it.

Nor did the unjust proceeding stop here. The Supreme Court confirmed the convictions secured by these iniquitous proceedings, and they confirmed it under a Constitution which declares, —

"All men have a natural and indefeasible right to worship Almighty God according to the dictates of their own consciences ; no man can of right be compelled to attend, erect, or support any place of worship, or to maintain any ministry against his consent. No human authority can, in any case or manner whatsoever, control or interfere with the right of conscience ; and no preference shall ever be given by law to any religious establishment, denomination, or mode of worship, above any other."

The concluding portion of the decision reads as follows : —

"The appellant's argument, then, is reduced to this: That because he conscientiously believes he is permitted by the law of God to labor on Sunday, he may violate with impunity the statute declaring it illegal to do so ; but a man's religious belief cannot be accepted as a justification for his committing an overt act made criminal by the law of the land. If the law operates harshly, as laws sometimes do, the remedy is in the hands of the legislature. It is not the province of the judiciary to pass upon the wisdom or policy of legislation. That is for the members of the legislative department; and the only appeal from their determination is to the constituency."

This decision of the Supreme Court is of the same piece with the prosecutions and judicial processes throughout. It gives to the legislature all the omnipotence of the British Parliament, and in that does away with all necessity for a Constitution. The decision on this principle alone is un-American. No legislative power in this country is framed upon the model of the British Parliament in respect to power. In this country, the powers of every legislature are defined and limited by Constitutions. It is the prerogative of Supreme Courts to define the meaning of the Constitution, and to decide whether an act of the legislature is Constitutional or not. If the act is Constitutional, then it must stand, whatever the results may be. And the Supreme Court is the body by which the Constitutionality or the unconstitutionality of any statute is to be discovered. But if, as this decision declares, the legislature is omnipotent, and that which it does must stand as law, then there is no use for a Constitution. "One of the objects for which the judiciary department is established, is the protection of the Constitutional rights of the citizens."

So long as there is a Constitution above the legislature, which defines and limits its powers, and protects and guards the rights of the citizens, so long it is the province of the Supreme Court to pronounce upon the acts of the legislature. The Supreme Court of Arkansas, therefore, in this case, clearly abdicated one of the very functions for which it was created, or else subverted the Constitution of Arkansas; and in either case, bestowed upon the legislature the omnipotence of the British Parliament, which is contrary to every principle of American institutions. Nor is the State of Arkansas an exception in this case, for this is the usual procedure of Supreme Courts in sustaining Sunday laws. They cannot be sustained upon any American principle ; resort has to be made in every instance, and has been with scarcely an exception, either to the church-and-State principles of the British Government, or to the British principle of the omnipotence of the legislative power. But American principles are far above and far in advance of the principles of the British Government, in that they recognize Constitutional limitations upon the legislative power, and countenance no union of church and State ; consequently, Sunday laws never have been, and never can be, sustained upon American principles.

That this indictment of the Supreme Court of Arkansas is not unjust, we have the clearest proof. The three judges who then composed the Supreme Court, were all members of the Bar Association of the State of Arkansas. In less than three months after this decision was rendered, the Bar Association unanimously made a report to the State on " law and law reform," an official copy of which we have in our possession. In that report, under the heading " Sunday Laws," is the following : —

"Our statute as it stands in Mansfield's Digest, provides that 'persons who are members of any religious society who observe as Sabbath any other day of the week than the Christian Sabbath, or Sunday, shall not be subject to the penalties of this act (the Sunday law), so that they observe one day in seven, agreeably to the faith and practice of their church or society.'— *Mans. Dig.*, sec. 1886.

"This statute had been in force from the time of the organization of the State government ; but it was unfortunately repealed by act of March 3, 1885.— *Acts 1885*, p. 37

" While the Jews adhere, of course, to the letter of the original command to remember the seventh day of the week, there is also in the State a small but respectable body of Christians who consistently believe that the seventh day is the proper day to be kept sacred ; and in the case of Scoles *vs.* State, our Supreme Court was compelled to affirm a judgment against a member of one of these churches, for worshiping God according to the dictates of his own conscience, supported, as he supposed, by good theological arguments. It is very evident that the system now in force, savoring as it does very much of religious persecution, is a relic of the Middle Ages, when it was thought that men could be made orthodox by an act of parliament. Even in Massachusetts, where Sabbatarian laws have always been enforced with unusual vigor, exceptions are made in favor of persons who religiously observe any other day in the place of Sunday. We think that the law as it stood in Mansfield's Digest, should be restored, with such an amendment as would prevent the sale of spirits on Sunday, as that was probably the object of repealing the above section."

Now the Arkansas Constitution says, " All men have a natural and indefeasible right to worship Almighty God according to the dictates of their own consciences." This report of the Bar Association says, " in the case of Scoles *vs.* State, our Supreme Court was compelled to affirm a judgment against a member of one of these churches, for worshiping God according to the dictates of his own conscience."

The members of the Supreme Court being members of the Bar Association, in that report it is confessed that they confirmed a judgment against a man for doing that which the Constitution explicitly declares all men have a natural and indefeasible right to do. By this, therefore, it is demonstrated that the men who composed the Supreme Court of Arkansas in 1885, plainly ignored the first principles of Constitutional law, as well as the express provisions of the Constitution they were sworn to uphold.

Just one more consideration, and we are done for this time. The form of indictment in all these cases, was the same as that printed on page 115.

Thus the State of Arkansas declared that for a man to work quietly and peaceably on his own premises on Sunday, digging potatoes, picking peaches, plowing, etc., is against the *peace* and *dignity* of the State of Arkansas. This relegates honest occupations to the realm of crime, peaceable employment to the realm of disorder, and puts a premium upon idleness and recklessness. When any State or body of people declares it to be against the dignity of that State or people for a man to follow any honest occupation on his own premises on any day, then we think the less dignity of that kind possessed, the better it will be for all concerned. And when such things are considered as offenses against the peace of any State or community, that State or community must be composed of most exceedingly irritable people.

The fact of the matter is, — and the whole history of these proceedings proves it, — from beginning to end these prosecutions were only the manifestation of that persecuting, intolerant spirit that will always make itself felt when any class of religionists can control the civil power. The information upon which the indictments were found, was treacherously given, and in the very spirit of the Inquisition. The indictment itself is a travesty of legal form, and a libel upon justice. The principle was more worthy of the Dark Ages than of any civilized nation or modern time ; and the Supreme Court decision that confirmed the convictions, rendered by judges who stultified themselves within three months, is one which, as we have shown, is contrary to the first principles of Constitutional law or Constitutional compacts. Nor is it certain that Arkansas was worse in these respects than any other State would be under like circumstances. Religious big-

ots in Arkansas are **no worse than** they would be in any
other State ; and if Congress should lend its sanction to
religious legislation **to the extent of** passing any such law
as the Blair **Sunday bill embodies, and** then **its** principles
should be made **of force in all** the States, the history **of**
Arkansas from 1885 to 1887 would be repeated throughout the whole extent of the nation.

In none of these cases have we given names with the intent of casting reflection upon any persons, except the "informers," but only that those who read the account may
have opportunity to verify the facts, if they choose. But in
the matter of the Supreme Court, our discussion of that decision is an intentional stricture, for the reasons given. Yet
we do not mean by so doing, to place the judges mentioned
in any more unenviable light than that in which the Supreme Courts of New York, Pennsylvania, and other
States stand. The principles of their decision have their
precedent in the decisions of these other States, and were
embodied in a dissenting opinion of one man who is now
an Associate-Justice of the United States Supreme Court,
given when he was a member of a State Supreme Court.

April 10, 1858, the legislature of California passed
"An act to provide for the better observance of the Sabbath." The Constitution of California declares that "the
free exercise and enjoyment of religious profession and
worship, without discrimination or preference, shall forever be allowed in this State." A Jew by the name of
Newman was convicted of selling goods on Sunday in
Sacramento. Upon his imprisonment, his case was
brought before the Supreme Court on a writ of *habeas
corpus*, on the ground of the illegality of his imprisonment,
because of the act's being unconstitutional. The majority
of the Supreme Court,— Judge Terry and Judge Burnett,—
sustained the plea by decisions separately written, whose
soundness, both upon Constitutional principles and upon

the abstract principle of justice itself, can never be successfully controverted. Stephen J Field, who is now Associate-Justice of the Supreme Court of the United States,
was then the third member of the Supreme Court of California. He rendered a dissenting opinion, taking the
identical position of the Arkansas Supreme Court as to
the omnipotence of the legislature, and soberly maintaining that the term "Christian Sabbath," used in the act,
was not a discrimination or preference in favor of any religious profession or worship.

The principles of this dissenting opinion, as of the
decision of the Supreme Court of Arkansas, are wholly
wrong, and spring from the principles of church and State,
and of the supremacy of the parliament of the British Government, and are totally subversive of American principles.

Yet, we repeat, Sunday laws have never been, and
never can be, sustained on any other principles; which is
only to say: There is no foundation in justice or in right
for any Sunday laws, or Sabbath laws, or Lord's day laws,
under any government on this earth.

CONGRESSIONAL REPORT — TRANSPORTATION OF
THE MAIL ON THE SABBATH.

As a fitting close to our discussion of this subject, we
insert a portion of the report of a United States Senate
committee on the same subject, sixty years ago — session
of 1828-29. The arguments are unanswerable; and the
principles stated are just now worthy of the most earnest
consideration of every American citizen : —

"The Senate proceeded to the consideration of the
following report and resolution, presented by Mr. Johnson, with which the Senate concurred : —

"'The committee to whom were referred the several
petitions on the subject of mails on the Sabbath, or first
day of the week, report, —

"'That some respite is required from the ordinary vocations of life, is an established principle, sanctioned by the usages of all nations, whether Christian or pagan. One day in seven has also been determined upon as the proportion of time ; and in conformity with the wishes of a great majority of the citizens of this country, the first day of the week, commonly called Sunday, has been set apart to that object. The principle has received the sanction of the national legislature, so far as to admit a suspension of all public business on that day, except in cases of absolute necessity, or of great public utility. This principle the committee would not wish to disturb. If kept within its legitimate sphere of action, no injury can result from its observance. It should, however, be kept in mind that *the proper object of government is to protect all persons in the enjoyment of their religious as well as civil rights, and not to determine for any whether they shall esteem one day above another, or esteem all days alike holy.*

"'We are aware that a variety of sentiment exists among the good citizens of this nation, on the subject of the Sabbath day ; and our Government is designed for the protection of one as much as another. The Jews, who in this country are as free as Christians, and entitled to the same protection from the laws, derive their obligation to keep the Sabbath day from the fourth commandment of their decalogue, and in conformity with that injunction, pay religious homage to the seventh day of the week, which we call Saturday. One denomination of Christians among us, justly celebrated for their piety, and certainly as good citizens as any other class, agree with the Jews in the moral obligation of the Sabbath, and observe the same day. . . . The Jewish Government was a theocracy, which enforced religious observances ; and though the committee would hope that no portion of the citizens of our country would willingly introduce a system of religious coercion in our civil institutions, the example of other nations should admonish us to watch carefully against its earliest indication. With these different religious views, the committee are of opinion that Congress cannot interfere. *It is not the legitimate province of the legislature to determine what religion is true, or what false.*

"'*Our Government is a civil, and not a religious, institution.* Our Constitution recognizes in every person the right to choose his own religion, and to enjoy it freely, without molestation. Whatever **may** be the religious **sentiments of** citizens, and however variant, they are alike entitled to protection from the Government, so long as they do not **invade the** rights **of others.** The transportation **of the mail on** the **first day of the** week, it is believed, **does not** interfere with **the rights of** conscience. *The petitioners for its discontinuance appear to be actuated by a religious zeal which may be commendable if confined to its proper sphere; but they assume a position better suited to an ecclesiastical than to a civil institution.* They appear in many instances to lay it down as an axiom, that the practice is a violation of the law of God. Should **Congress** in legislative capacity adopt the sentiment, it would establish the principle that the legislature is a proper tribunal to determine what are the laws of God. It would **involve a legislative decision on a religious** controversy, **and on a point in which good** citizens may honestly differ **in** opinion, without disturbing the peace of society or endangering **its** liberties. **If** this principle is once introduced, **it** will be impossible **to** define its bounds.

"'*Among all the religious persecutions* **with which** **almost** *every page* **of** *modern history is* **stained, no victim** *ever suffered but for the violation of what government denominated the law of* **God.** To prevent a similar train of evils in this country, **the Constitution** has wisely withheld from our Government **the power of** defining the divine law. It is a right reserved **to each citizen** ; and while he respects the rights of others, **he cannot be** held amenable to any human tribunal **for his conclusions.** *Extensive religious combinations to effect a political* **object,** *are, in the opinion of the committee, always dangerous.* This first effort of the kind calls for the establishment of **a** principle, which, in the opinion **of** the committee, **would** lay the foundation for dangerous innovations upon the spirit of the Constitution, and upon the religious rights of the citizens. *If admitted, it may be justly apprehended that the future measures of* **the** *Government will be strongly marked, if not eventually controlled, by the same influence. All religious despotism commences by combination and influence,* *and when that influence begins* **to** *operate upon the political institutions of a country, the civil power soon bends under it; and the* **catastrophe** *of other nations furnishes an awful warning* **of the** *consequence.*

"'While the mail is transported **on** Saturday, the **Jew and** the Sabbatarian may abstain from any agency in carrying it, **on** conscientious scruples. While it is transported **on** the first day of the week, another class may abstain, from the same religious scruples. The obligation of Government is the same on both these classes; and the committee can discover no principle on which the claims of one should be more respected than those of the other, *unless it be admitted that the consciences of* **the minority** *are less sacred than those of the majority.*

"'If the **observance** of a holy **day becomes incorporated** in our institutions, shall we not forbid the movement of an army, prohibit an assault in time of war, and lay an injunction upon our naval officers to lie in the wind while upon **the ocean on** that day? Consistency would seem to require **it. Nor is it** certain that we should stop **here.** *If the principle is* **once** *established that religion, or religious observances, shall be interwoven with our legislative acts, we must pursue it to its ultimatum.* We shall, if consistent, provide for the erection of edifices for worship of the Creator, and for the support of Christian ministers, if we believe such measures will promote the **interests** of Christianity.* It is the settled conviction **of the committee,** that the only method of avoiding **these** consequences, with their attendant train of evils, **is to** adhere

---

* **This** is precisely what the National Reform Association proposes to do when religious legislation is once recognized. In the *Christian Statesman* of Feb. 21, 1884, Rev. J. M. Foster, a "district secretary" of the National Reform Association, declared that among the duties which the reigning Mediator requires **of nations, is** "an acknowledgment and performance of the nation's duty to guard and protect the church by suppressing **all** public violation of the moral law, . . by exempting **church property from** taxation," and "*by providing her funds out of* **the public treasury,** for carrying on her aggressive work at home and in the foreign field." The Scripture says, "God hath ordained that they which **preach** the gospel shall **live of** the gospel;" but **these** men propose to ordain that they which preach the gospel shall live of the law, through **the** public treasury.

strictly to the spirit of the Constitution, which regards the general Government in no other light than that of a civil institution, wholly destitute of religious authority. *What other nations call religious toleration, we call religious rights. They are not exercised in virtue of governmental indulgence, but as rights, of which Government cannot deprive any portion of citizens, however small. Despotic power may invade those rights, but justice still confirms them.*

"'Let the national legislature once perform an act which involves the decision of a religious controversy, and it will have passed its legitimate bounds. The precedent will then be established, and the foundation laid, for that usurpation of the divine prerogative in this country which has been the desolating scourge to the fairest portion of the Old World.

"'Our Constitution recognizes no other power than that of persuasion, for enforcing religious observances. Let the professors of Christianity recommend their religion by deeds of benevolence, by Christian meekness, by lives of temperance and holiness. Let them combine their efforts to instruct the ignorant, to relieve the widow and the orphan, to promulgate to the world the gospel of their Saviour, recommending its precepts by their habitual example; Government will find its legitimate object in protecting them. It cannot oppose them, and they will not need its aid. *Their moral influence will then do infinitely more to advance the true interests of religion, than any measure which they may call on Congress to enact.* The petitioners do not complain of any infringement upon their own rights. They enjoy all that Christians ought to ask at the hands of any Government — protection from all molestation in the exercise of their religious sentiments.'

"*Resolved*, That the committee be discharged from any further consideration of the subject."

APPENDIX A.

WE here append some statements of prominent citizens of Arkansas, who are not observers of the seventh day, in relation to the workings of that Sunday law, which show that our report of the cases is not "manufactured" in any particular.

We first give in full a statement from Judge S. W. Williams, of Little Rock, an ex-judge of the State Supreme Court, and one of the foremost lawyers in the State : —

LITTLE ROCK, ARK., March 21, 1887.

Rev. Dan. T. Jones,   .

SIR : As requested, I give you a short *resume* of the history of our Sabbath law of 1885. Up to the time of the meeting of the legislature in January, 1885, our Sunday law had always excepted from its sanctions the cases wherein persons from conscience kept the seventh day as the Sabbath. It had been the case for many years at the capital, that no Sabbath laws were observed by the saloon-keepers. After the election of 1884, the newly elected prosecuting attorney of that district, commenced a rigid enforcement of the law. A few Jewish saloon-keepers successfully defied it during the session of the legislature. This led to the total and unqualified repeal of the conscience proviso for the seventh day in the old law. This was used oppressively upon the seventh-day Sabbath Christians, to an extent that shocked the bar of the whole State. A test case was brought from Washington County. Our Supreme Court could not see its way clear to hold the law unconstitutional, but the judges, as

men and lawyers, abborred it. Judge B. B. Battle, one
of the three judges, was, with Judge Rose and myself, a
member of the standing committee on law reform of our
State Bar Association. In our report, as you see, we
recommended a change, which the Association adopted
unanimously, Chief-Justice Cockrill and Associate-Jus-
tices Smith and Battle being members, present and voting. At the meeting of the General Assembly the next
week (January, 1887), Senator Crockett introduced a bill
repealing the obnoxious law, in so far as it affected those
who keep holy the seventh day, still forbidding the opening of saloons on Sunday.   Truly yours,
                                    SAM. W. WILLIAMS.

In the following letter, Judge U. M. Rose, of the law
firm of U. M. & G. B. Rose, Little Rock, one of the leading lawyers in the State, and a member of the committee
on law reform of the State Bar Association, gives his
opinion of the reasons why tlre law was enacted, and also
his views as a lawyer on the propriety of such legislation.
We print his letter in full : —

                     · LITTLE ROCK, ARK., April 15, 1887.
Rev. Dan. T. Jones,
        Springdale, Ark.,
    DEAR SIR : Yours received. The law passed in this
State in 1885, and which has since been repealed, requiring all persons to keep Sunday as a day of rest, although
they might religiously keep some other day of the week,
was enacted, I think, to meet the case of certain Jews in
this city who kept saloons and other business houses open
on Sunday. It was said that those persons only made a
pretense of keeping Saturday as a day of rest. Whether
these statements were true or not, I do not know. The
act of 1885 was found to work oppressively on persons
believing as you do that Saturday is the Christian as well
as the Jewish Sabbath ; and hence its repeal. It was
manifestly unjust to them as well as to Jews who are
sincere in their faith.
    You ask me to express my opinion as to the propriety
of such legislation as that contained in the repealed act.

Nothing can exceed my abhorrence for any kind of legislation that has for its object the restraint of any class of men in the exercise of their own religious opinions. It is the fundamental basis of our Government that every man shall be allowed to worship God according to the dictates of his own conscience. It was certainly not a little singular, that while in our churches the command was regularly read at stated times, requiring all men to keep the Sabbath, which, amongst the Jews to whom the command was addressed, was the seventh day of the week, men should be prosecuted and convicted in the courts for doing so. As to the theological aspect of the matter, I am not competent to speak; but as a civil requirement, my opinion is that any legislation that attempts to control the consciences of men as to the discharge of religious duty, can only be the result of that ignorance and fanaticism which for centuries proved to be the worst curse that ever afflicted humanity.   Very respectfully yours,

U. M. ROSE.

Mr. E. Stinson is a farmer and teacher in Hot Spring County, and writes:—

MALCOLM, HOT SPRING CO., ARK., March 27, 1887.

Mr. Jones,

DEAR SIR: In answer to your inquiry, will say that since the repeal of the exemption clause in our statutes, which allowed persons who kept another day than Sunday as Sabbath, to go about their ordinary work or business on that day, several indictments have been found in Hot Spring County. In each and every case the parties so indicted have been conscientious observers of the seventh day, so far as I know them. To my knowledge, others have worked on Sunday who did not observe the seventh day, and no bills were found against them. I believe the prosecutions to be more for religious persecution than for the purpose of guarding the Sunday from desecration. The men who have been indicted are all good moral men and law-abiding citizens, to the best of my knowledge. The indictments, to the best of my belief, were malicious in their character, and without provocation. I believe the unmodified Sunday law to be unjust in its nature, and that it makes an unjust discrimination against a small but worthy class of our citizens. I am a member of the Baptist Church, and not an observer of the seventh day ; but I accept with gratitude the recent change in the laws of our State, which shows more respect for the conscientious convictions of all our citizens. I do not believe that if the same acts for which the indictments were lodged against Seventh-Day Adventists, had been committed by those who did not keep the seventh day, any notice would have been taken of them.

Respectfully,

E. STINSON.

We present in full a letter from the physician and the proprietor of the Potash Sulphur Springs Hotel, a health resort seven miles southeast of Hot Springs. These gentlemen are both old residents of the place, and are personally acquainted with some of those who were convicted of Sabbath-breaking in Hot Spring County.

POTASH SULPHUR SPRINGS, ARK., March, 1887.

To whom it may concern : —

We, the undersigned, herewith testify that the recent prosecutions against the observers of the seventh-day Sabbath in our vicinity, have brought to the surface a religious intolerance and a spirit of persecution, the existence whereof a great many imagine not to exist any more in our time.   J. T. FAIRCHILD, M. D.

E. E. WOODCOCK.

Another letter, from Mr. Fitzhugh, a Justice of the Peace, and acting deputy-sheriff in Hot Spring County during the two years in which the unmodified Sunday law was in force, will show the estimate as citizens and neighbors, placed upon some who were indicted for Sabbath-breaking.

STATE OF ARKANSAS, COUNTY OF HOT SPRING,

SALIM TOWNSHIP, April 9, 1887.

On the second day of March, 1885, the legislature of Arkansas repealed the law allowing any person to observe

.s the Sabbath any day of the week that they preferred, and compelled them to keep the Christian Sabbath, or first day of the week. The effect of this change worked a hardship on a class of citizens in this county, known as Seventh-day Adventists, who observe the seventh instead of the first day of the week, as the Lord's Sabbath. There were five or six of them indicted (and some of them the second time) by the Grand Jury of this county, for the violation of this law. In fact, these people were the only ones that were indicted for Sabbath-breaking, during the two years in which this law was in force. I was not intimately acquainted with but one of these people, Mr. John Shockey, who moved from Ohio, and settled within one and one fourth miles of me, some two and a half years ago. I know nothing in the character of this gentleman but what would recommend him to the world at large. As a citizen, he recognizes and regards the laws of our country (with the above exception) ; as a neighbor, he might well be called a Samaritan ; as a Christian, he is strict to his profession, and proves his faith by his works.

Respectfully,

BENJ. C. FITZHUGH, *Justice of the Peace.*

Malvern, Hot Spring Co., **Ark.**

APPENDIX B.

AT the National Sunday-law convention held in **Washington**, D. C., Dec. 11–13, 1888, the original Blair Sunday bill was discussed by the preachers, with Mrs. J. Ellen Foster **as** legal **adviser**, and the following changes were proposed, and **unanimously** adopted Dec. 12. This is from the official **record**. The changes are indicated by stars and bold-faced **letters**.

" A Bill **to** secure **to the people** the enjoyment of the **Lord's day, commonly known as Sunday,** as a day of rest, and to **protect** its observance **as a day of** religious worship.

" *Be it enacted by the Senate and House of Representatives of the United States of America in Congress assembled,* That **on Sunday,** no person or corporation, or the agent, servant, **or** employee of **any person** or corporation, shall perform, **or** authorize **to be** performed, any secular work, labor, or business, * * * works of necessity, mercy, and humanity excepted ; **nor** shall any person engage in any play, game, **show, exhibition,** or amusement * * * **open to the public, or of a public character,** in any Territory, district, vessel, **or** place subject **to** the exclusive jurisdiction of the United States ; **nor** shall **it** be lawful **for** any person **or corporation to receive pay** for labor or serv-**ice** performed or rendered **in violation of** this section.

" SEC. 2. **That** no mails **or mail matter shall** hereafter be transported in time of peace over any land postal-route, nor shall any mail matter be collected, assorted, handled, or delivered during any part of Sunday.

"SEC. 3. That the prosecution of commerce between the States and with the Indian tribes, * * * by the transportation of persons or property by land or water * * * on the first day of the week, * * * is hereby prohibited, and any person or corporation, or the agent, servant, or employee of any person or corporation, who shall * * * violate this section, shall be punished by a fine of not less than ten nor more than one thousand dollars, and no service performed in the prosecution of such prohibited commerce shall be lawful, nor shall any compensation be recoverable or be paid for the same.

.   .   .   .

"SEC. 6. That labor or service performed and rendered on Sunday in consequence of accident, disaster, or unavoidable delays in making the regular connections upon postal-routes and routes of travel and transportation, the * * * transportation and delivery of milk before 5 A. M. and after 10 P. M., * * * shall not be deemed violations of this act, but the same shall be construed, so far as possible, to secure to the whole people rest from toil during Sunday, their mental and moral culture, and the protection of the religious observance of the * * * day."

The reasons for the changes asked are, in part, as follows : —

"For religious purposes we prefer the name *Lord's day* or *Christian Sabbath* but as *Sunday* is already used in national laws, we think it better to use that uniformly in this bill, with the one exception of the double name in the title.

"The word *promote* in the title goes beyond what many, even Christian citizens, believe to be the proper function of government with reference to 'religious worship,' while the word *protect* (see also last line) expresses a duty which government owes to all legitimate institutions of the people.

"Experience in the courts has shown that the words *show* and *exhibition* should be added to the list of prohibited Sunday amusements, and the words *in public*, in

place of *to the disturbance of others*, as the latter clause
has been construed as requiring that persons living in the
neighborhood of a Sunday game or show must testify
that they have been disturbed, in order to a conviction,
which cannot be done in some cases without personal
peril.

"In Section 2, we believe that the exceptions for
letters relating to sickness, etc., are unnecessary in this
age of the telegraph; and that they would be used by
unscrupulous men in business correspondence, and that
this would destroy most of the benefits of the law in its
bearing on Sunday mails.

"In Section 3, we believe the exceptions made would
greatly interfere with the administration of the law. The
exception for work of mercy and necessity is made, once
for all, in the first section. The reference to 'the disturbance of others' is objectionable for reasons already
given, and the word *willfully* is an old offender in Sabbath legislation, and requires evidence very hard to get
in regard to one's motive and knowledge of the law. In
other laws it is assumed that one knows the law, and the
law-making power should see that the laws are well published, and leave no room for one to escape by agnosti-
cism.

"In Section 3 (as in Section 1 also), we would omit the
words *Lord's day*, and in Section 6, *Sabbath*, in order to
preserve uniformity in using the less religious term *Sunday*.

"In Section 6, we think refrigerator cars make Sunday
work in transportation of perishable food, except milk,
unnecessary, and the new stock-cars, with provision for
food and water, do the same for stock-trains. So many
of the State Sunday laws have proved almost useless in
protecting the rights of the people to Sunday rest and
undisturbed worship, by the smallness of their penalties
and the largeness of their exceptions, that we covet from
Congress a law that shall make itself effective by small
exceptions and large penalties."

With a little care in comparison, the reader can readily
see what changes have been made in the bill. We have
omitted Sections 4 and 5 from the revised bill, because

they are the same as the corresponding sections in the
original bill, with the single exception that the word
Sunday is substituted for *Lord's day*, in the last line of
Section 4. We hope that every one will study both bills
thoroughly, together with the committee's reasons for the
changes. Any one can see that the changes are in the
line of greater stringency. We note only the most prominent points.

1. The change from *Lord's day* to *Sunday*, although a
proper one, is in reality no change at all, since the term
Lord's day is still used at the beginning, and it is expressly stated that *Sunday* is used only as a matter of
custom. It is understood that it is as a *religious* day,
indicated by the term *Lord's day*, that they want the
observance of the first day of the week enforced ; but if
the term *Sunday* is quite generally used, it will, no doubt,
" take " better.

2. In asking for the "*protection* of the religious observance of the day," instead of the *promotion* of its observance as a day of religious worship, the committee
threw a sop to those who are "on the fence" in regard
to religious legislation. As it stands, it amounts to nothing ; for there is not a State or Territory in the Union
where any religious service held on Sunday would not
be protected.

3. The most important change of all, however, is the
substitution of the words *in public* for *to the disturbance
of others*, in Section 1. This will certainly make the law
more effective. It is obvious that if a man were to engage
in work a mile from a dwelling-house, it would be quite a
task for the owner of the house to convince even an
ordinary jury that such labor disturbed him ; but by the
terms of the amended bill, the man may be convicted if
he is working in a public place, provided anybody can
get near enough to him to see him.

4. Notice the radical change made in Section 2. As amended, it is most sweeping, allowing of no exception. The mail is not to be carried at all on Sunday, even in cases of sickness and death, lest some "unscrupulous" person should mention business on that day. If the mail is not carried, of course that will make him a good man! It is no concern of ours how they propose to carry out this law, but we can't help wondering what they will do when Sunday comes, and a train carrying the mail is on the way from one city to another within the same State, say from San Francisco to Los Angeles. The train is owned by a corporation, and is not in a part of the country "subject to the exclusive jurisdiction of the United States," and therefore could not be forced to lie over. The only way out of the difficulty, under the provision of this bill, would be to dump all the mail out at the nearest station, and let it lie there till Sunday was past.

This, however, would not be done. What would be done, would be the passing of laws by the several States, forbidding all labor within their jurisdiction; and it is this for which these zealous people are scheming. This United States law is designed as a precedent, and as a lever with which to secure the religious observance of Sunday by all the people in the United States, whether they are religious or not.

5. We wish to call special attention, also, to the last sentence of the "reason for the changes asked." It says: "So many of the State Sunday laws have proved almost useless in protecting the rights of the people to Sunday rest and undisturbed worship, by the smallness of their penalties and the largeness of their exceptions, that we covet from Congress a law that shall make itself effective by *small exceptions and large penalties.*" There the real spirit of the dragon exhibits itself. In that simple statement is compressed a world of bigotry and animosity.

APPENDIX C.

THE DECLARATION OF INDEPENDENCE.

WHEN, in the course of human events, it becomes necessary for one people to dissolve the political bands which have connected them with another, and to assume, among the powers of the earth, the separate and equal station to which the laws of nature and of nature's God entitle them, a decent respect to the opinions of mankind requires that they should declare the causes which impel them to the separation.

We hold these truths to be self-evident, that all men are created equal; that they are endowed by their Creator with certain unalienable rights; that among these are life, liberty, and the pursuit of happiness. That to secure these rights, governments are instituted among men, deriving their just powers from the consent of the governed; that whenever any form of government becomes destructive of these ends, it is the right of the people to alter or to abolish it, and to institute a new government, laying its foundation on such principles, and organizing its powers in such form, as to them shall seem most likely to effect their safety and happiness. Prudence, indeed, will dictate that governments long established, should not be changed for light and transient causes; and accordingly, all experience hath shown that mankind are more disposed to suffer, while evils are sufferable, than to right themselves by abolishing the forms to which they are accustomed. But when a long train of abuses and usurpations, pursuing invariably the same object, evinces a design to reduce them under absolute despotism, it is their right, it is their duty, to throw off such government, and to provide new guards for their future security. Such has been the patient sufferance of these Colonies, and such is now the necessity which constrains them to alter their former systems of government. The history of the present king of Great Britain, is a history of repeated injuries and usurpations, all having, in direct object, the establishment of an absolute tyranny over these States. To prove this, let facts be submitted to a candid world : —

He has refused his assent to laws the most wholesome and necessary for the public good.

He has forbidden his Governors to pass laws of immediate and pressing importance, unless suspended in their operation till his assent should be obtained ; and, when so suspended, he has utterly neglected to attend to them.

He has refused to pass other laws for the accommodation of large districts of people, unless those people would relinquish the right of representation in the legislature ; a right inestimable to them, and formidable to tyrants only.

He has called together legislative bodies at places unusual, uncomfortable, and distant from the depository of their public records, for the sole purpose of fatiguing them into compliance with his measures.

He has dissolved representative houses repeatedly, for opposing, with manly firmness, his invasions on the rights of the people.

He has refused, for a long time after such dissolutions, to cause others to be elected ; whereby the legislative powers, incapable of annihilation, have returned to the people at large for their exercise ; the State remaining, in the meantime, exposed to all the danger of invasion from without, and convulsions within.

He has endeavored to prevent the population of these States ; for that purpose obstructing the laws for the naturalization of foreigners, refusing to pass others to encourage their migration hither, and raising the conditions of new appropriations of lands.

He has obstructed the administration of justice, by refusing his assent to laws for establishing judiciary powers.

He has made judges dependent on his will alone for the tenure of their offices, and the amount and payment of their salaries.

He has erected a multitude of new offices, and sent hither swarms of officers to harass our people and eat out their substance.

He has kept among us, in times of peace, standing armies, without the consent of our legislature.

He has affected to render the military independent of, and superior to, the civil power.

He has combined, with others, to subject us to a jurisdiction foreign to our Constitution, and unacknowledged by our laws ; giving his assent to their acts of pretended legislation.

For quartering large bodies of armed troops among us :

For protecting them, by a mock trial, from punishment for any murders which they should commit on the inhabitants of these States :

For cutting off our trade with all parts of the world :

For imposing taxes on us without our consent :

For depriving us, in many cases, of the benefits of trial by jury :

For transporting us beyond seas to be tried for pretended offenses :

For abolishing the free system of English laws in a neighboring province, establishing therein an arbitrary government, and enlarging its boundaries, so as to render it at once an example and fit instrument for introducing the same absolute rule into these Colonies :

For taking away our charters, abolishing our most valuable laws, and altering, fundamentally, the powers of our governments :

For suspending our own legislatures, and declaring themselves invested with power to legislate for us in all cases whatsoever.

He has abdicated government here, by declaring us out of his protection, and waging war against us.

He has plundered our seas, ravaged our coasts, burnt our towns, and destroyed the lives of our people.

He is, at this time, transporting large armies of foreign mercenaries to complete the works of death, desolation, and tyranny, already begun, with circumstances of cruelty and perfidy scarcely paralleled in the most barbarous ages, and totally unworthy the head of a civilized nation.

He has constrained our fellow-citizens, taken captive on the high seas, to bear arms against their country, to become the executioners of their friends and brethren, or to fall themselves by their hands.

He has excited domestic insurrections among us, and has endeavored to bring on the inhabitants of our frontiers the merciless Indian savages, whose known rule of warfare is an undistinguished destruction of all ages, sexes, and conditions.

In every stage of these oppressions, we have petitioned for redress in the most humble terms; our repeated petitions have been answered only by repeated injury. A prince whose character is thus marked by every act which may define a tyrant, is unfit to be the ruler of a free people.

Nor have we been wanting in attention to our British brethren. We have warned them, from time to time, of attempts made by their legislature to extend an unwarrantable jurisdiction over us. We have reminded them of the circumstances of our emigration and settlement here. We have appealed to their native justice and magnanimity, and we have conjured them, by the ties of our common kindred, to disavow these usurpations, which would inevitably interrupt our connections and correspondence. They, too, have been deaf to the voice of justice and consanguinity. We must, therefore, acquiesce in the necessity which denounces our separation, and hold them, as we hold the rest of mankind, enemies in war, in peace friends.

We, therefore, the Representatives of the United States of America, in General Congress assembled, appealing to the Supreme Judge of the world for the rectitude of our intentions, do, in the name and by the authority of the good people of these Colonies, solemnly publish and declare, That these United Colonies are, and, of right, ought to be, *free and independent States ;* that they are absolved from all allegiance to the British crown, and that all political connection between them and the State of Great Britain is, and ought to be, totally dissolved ; and that, as *free and independent States*, they have full power to levy war, conclude peace, contract alliances, establish commerce, and to do all other acts and things which *independent States* may of right do. And, for the support of this Declaration, with a firm reliance on the protection of Divine Providence, we mutually pledge to each other our lives, our fortunes, and our sacred honor.

Massachusetts Bay.

JOHN HANCOCK,
SAMUEL ADAMS,
JOHN ADAMS,
ROBERT TREAT PAINE,
ELBRIDGE GERRY.

New Hampshire.

JOSIAH BARTLETT,
WILLIAM WHIPPLE,
MATTHEW THORNTON.

Rhode Island.

STEPHEN HOPKINS,
WILLIAM ELLERY.

New York.

WILLIAM FLOYD,
PHILIP LIVINGSTON,
FRANCIS LEWIS,
LEWIS MORRIS.

New Jersey.

RICHARD STOCKTON,
JOHN WITHERSPOON,
FRANCIS HOPKINSON,
JOHN HART,
ABRAHAM CLARK.

Pennsylvania.

ROBERT MORRIS,
BENJAMIN RUSH,
BENJAMIN FRANKLIN,
JOHN MORTON,
GEORGE CLYMER,
JAMES SMITH,
GEORGE TAYLOR,
JAMES WILSON,
GEORGE ROSS.

Connecticut.

ROGER SHERMAN,
SAMUEL HUNTINGTON,
WILLIAM WILLIAMS,
OLIVER WOLCOTT.

Delaware.

CÆSAR RODNEY,
GEORGE READ,
THOMAS M'KEAN.

Maryland.

SAMUEL CHASE,
WILLIAM PACA,
THOMAS STONE,
CHARLES CARROLL, of Carrollton.

Virginia.

GEORGE WYTHE,
RICHARD HENRY LEE,
THOMAS JEFFERSON,
BENJAMIN HARRISON,
THOMAS NELSON, JUN.,
FRANCIS LIGHTFOOT LEE,
CARTER BRAXTON.

North Carolina.

WILLIAM HOOPER,
JOSEPH HEWES,
JOHN PENN.

South Carolina.

EDWARD RUTLEDGE,
THOMAS HEYWARD, JUN.,
THOMAS LYNCH, JUN.,
ARTHUR MIDDLETON.

Georgia.

BUTTON GWINNETT,
LYMAN HALL,
GEORGE WALTON.

APPENDIX D.

THE CONSTITUTION OF THE UNITED STATES.

WE, the people of the United States, in order to form a more perfect union, establish justice, insure domestic tranquillity, provide for the common defense, promote the general welfare, and secure the blessings of liberty to ourselves and our posterity, do ordain and establish this Constitution for the United States of America.

ARTICLE 1.

SECTION I. All legislative powers herein granted shall be vested in a Congress of the United States, which shall consist of a Senate and House of Representatives.

SEC. 2. The House of Representatives shall be composed of members chosen every second year by the people of the several States, and the electors in each State shall have the qualifications requisite for electors of the most numerous branch of the State legislature.

No person shall be a representative who shall not have attained to the age of twenty-five years, and been seven years a citizen of the United States, and who shall not, when elected, be an inhabitant of that State in which he shall be chosen.

Representatives and direct taxes shall be apportioned among the several States which may be included within this Union, according to their respective numbers, which shall be determined by adding to the whole number of free persons, including those bound to service for a term of years, and excluding Indians not taxed, three fifths of all other persons. The actual enumeration shall be made within three years after the first meeting of the Congress of the United States, and within every subsequent term of ten years, in such manner as they shall by law direct. The number of representatives shall not exceed one for every thirty thousand, but each State shall have at least one representative; and until such enumeration shall be made, the State of New Hampshire shall be entitled to choose three; Massachusetts, eight; Rhode Island and Providence Plantations, one; Connecticut, five; New York, six; New Jersey, four; Pennsylvania, eight; Delaware, one; Maryland, six; Virginia, ten; North Carolina, five; South Carolina, five; and Georgia, three.

When vacancies happen in the representation from any State, the executive authority thereof shall issue writs of election to fill such vacancies.

The House of Representatives shall chose their Speaker and other officers, and shall have the sole power of impeachment.

SEC. 3. The Senate of the United States shall be composed of two senators from each State, chosen by the legislature thereof, for six years; and each senator shall have one vote.

Immediately after they shall be assembled in consequence of the first election, they shall be divided as equally as may be into three classes. The seats of the senators of the first class shall be vacated at the expiration of the second year; of the second class, at the expiration of the fourth year; and of the third class, at the expiration of the sixth year, so that one third may be chosen every second year; and if vacancies happen by resignation, or otherwise, during the recess of the legislature of any State, the executive thereof may make temporary appointments until the next meeting of the legislature, which shall then fill such vacancies.

No person shall be a senator who shall not have attained to the age of thirty years, and been nine years a citizen of the United States, and who shall not, when elected, be an inhabitant of that State for which he shall be chosen.

The Vice-President of the United States shall be president of the Senate, but shall have no vote, unless they be equally divided.

The Senate shall choose their other officers, and also a president *pro tempore*, in the absence of the Vice-President, or when he shall exercise the office of President of the United States.

The Senate shall have the sole power to try all impeachments. When sitting for that purpose, they shall be on oath or affirmation. When the President of the United States is tried, the Chief-Justice shall preside. And no person shall be convicted without the concurrence of two thirds of the members present.

Judgment in cases of impeachment shall not extend further than to removal from office, and disqualification to hold and enjoy any office of honor, trust, or profit under the United States; but the party convicted shall nevertheless be liable and subject to indictment, trial, judgment, and punishment, according to law.

SEC. 4. The times, places, and manner of holding elections for senators and representatives shall be prescribed in each State by the legislature thereof; but the Congress may at any time, by law, make or alter such regulations, except as to the places of choosing senators.

The Congress shall assemble at least once in every year, and such meeting shall be on the first Monday in December, unless they shall, by law, appoint a different day.

SEC. 5. Each house shall be the judge of the elections, returns, and qualifications of its own members, and a majority of each shall constitute a quorum to do business; but a smaller number may adjourn from day to day, and be authorized to compel the attendance of absent members, in such manner and under such penalties as each house may provide.

Each house may determine the rules of its proceedings, punish its members for disorderly behavior, and, with the concurrence of two thirds, expel a member.

Each house shall keep a journal of its proceedings, and from time to time publish the same, excepting such parts as may in their judgment require secrecy; and the yeas and nays of the members of either house on any question shall, at the desire of one fifth of those present, be entered on the journal.

Neither house, during the session of Congress, shall, without the consent of the other, adjourn for more than three days, nor to any other place than that in which the two houses shall be sitting.

SEC. 6. The senators and representatives shall receive a compensation for their services, to be ascertained by law, and paid out of the treasury of the United States. They shall in all cases, except treason, felony, and breach of the peace, be privileged from arrest during their attendance at the session of their respective houses, and in going to and returning from the same; and for any speech or debate in either house they shall not be questioned in any other place.

No senator or representative shall, during the time for which he was elected, be appointed to any civil office under the authority of the United States, which shall have been created, or the emoluments whereof shall have been increased, during such time; and no person holding any office under the United States shall be a member of either house during his continuance in office.

SEC. 7. All bills for raising revenue shall originate in the House of Representatives; but the Senate may propose or concur with amendments, as on other bills.

Every bill which shall have passed the House of Representatives and the Senate, shall, before it become a law, be presented to the President of the United States; if he approve, he shall sign it; but if not, he shall return it, with his objections, to that house in which it shall have originated, who shall enter the objections at large on their journal, and proceed to reconsider it. If after such reconsideration two thirds of that house shall agree to pass the bill, it shall be sent, together with the objections, to the other house, by which it shall likewise be reconsidered; and if approved by two thirds of that house, it shall become a law. But in all such cases, the votes of both houses shall be determined by yeas and nays, and the names of the persons voting for and against the bill shall be entered on the journal of each house respectively. If any bill shall not be returned by the President within ten days (Sunday excepted) after it shall have been presented to him, the same shall be a law in like manner as if he had signed it, unless the Congress by their adjournment prevent its return; in which case it shall not be a law.

Every order, resolution, or vote to which the concurrence of the Senate and the House of Representatives may be necessary (except on a question of adjournment) shall be presented to the President of the United States; and before the same shall take effect, shall be approved by him, or, being disapproved

by him, shall be repassed by two thirds of the Senate and House of Repre
sentatives, according to the rules and limitations prescribed in the case of a
bill.

Sec. 8. The Congress shall have power—

To lay and collect taxes, duties, imposts, and excises, to pay the debts and
provide for the common defense and general welfare of the United States ; but
all duties, imposts, and excises shall be uniform throughout the United States ;

To borrow money on the credit of the United States ;

To regulate commerce with foreign nations, and among the several States,
and with the Indian tribes ;

To establish a uniform rule of naturalization, and uniform laws on the subject of bankruptcies throughout the United States ;

To coin money, regulate the value thereof, and of foreign coin, and fix the
standard of weights and measures ;

To provide for the punishment of counterfeiting the securities and current
coin of the United States ;

To establish post-offices and post-roads ;

To promote the progress of science and useful arts, by securing, for limited
times, to authors and inventors, the exclusive right to their respective writings
and discoveries ;

To constitute tribunals inferior to the Supreme Court ;

To define and punish piracies and felonies committed on the high seas, and
offenses against the law of nations ;

To declare war, grant letters of marque and reprisal, and make rules concerning captures on land and water ;

To raise and support armies, but no appropriation of money to that use shall
be for a longer term than two years ;

To provide and maintain a navy ;

To make rules for the government and regulation of the land and naval
forces ;

To provide for calling forth the militia to execute the laws of the Union,
suppress insurrections, and repel invasions ;

To provide for organizing, arming, and disciplining the militia, and for
governing such part of them as may be employed in the service of the United
States, reserving to the States respectively the appointment of the officers, and
the authority of training the militia according to the discipline prescribed by
Congress;

To exercise exclusive legislation in all cases whatsoever over such district (not
exceeding ten miles square) as may, by cession of particular States, and the
acceptance of Congress, become the seat of the Government of the United States,
and to exercise like authority over all places purchased by the consent of the
legislature of the State in which the same shall be, for the erection of forts,
magazines, arsenals, dock-yards, and other needful buildings ; and—

To make all laws which shall be necessary and proper for carrying into
execution the foregoing powers, and all other power vested by this Constitu-

tion in the Government of the United States, or in any department or officer thereof.

SEC. 9. The migration or importation of such persons as any of the States now existing shall think proper to admit, shall not be prohibited by the Congress prior to the year one thousand eight hundred and eight, but a tax or duty may be imposed on such importation, not exceeding ten dollars for each person.

The privilege of the writ of *habeas corpus* shall not be suspended, unless when in cases of rebellion or invasion the public safety may require it.

No bill of attainder or *ex post facto* law shall be passed.

No capitation or other direct tax shall be laid, unless in proportion to the census or enumeration hereinbefore directed to be taken.

No tax or duty shall be laid on articles exported from any State.

No preference shall be given by any regulation of commerce or revenue to the ports of one State over those of another; nor shall vessels bound to or from one State, be obliged to enter, clear, or pay duties in another.

No money shall be drawn from the treasury, but in consequence of appropriations made by law; and a regular statement and account of the receipts and expenditures of all public money shall be published from time to time.

No title of nobility shall be granted by the United States; and no person holding any office of profit or trust under them, shall, without the consent of the Congress, accept of any present, emolument, office, or title, of any kind whatever, from any king, prince, or foreign State.

SEC. 10. No State shall enter into any treaty, alliance, or confederation; grant letters of marque and reprisal; coin money; emit bills of credit; make anything but gold and silver coin a tender in payment of debts; pass any bill of attainder, *ex post facto* law, or law impairing the obligation of contracts, or grant any title of nobility.

No State shall, without the consent of the Congress, lay any imposts or duties on imports or exports, except what may be absolutely necessary for executing its inspection laws; and the net produce of all duties and imposts laid by any State on imports or exports, shall be for the use of the treasury of the United States; and all such laws shall be subject to the revision and control of the Congress.

No State shall, without the consent of Congress, lay any duty on tonnage, keep troops or ships of war in time of peace, enter into any agreement or compact with another State, or with a foreign power, or engage in war, unless actually invaded, or in such imminent danger as will not admit of delay.

ARTICLE II.

SECTION 1. The executive power shall be vested in a President of the United States of America. He shall hold his office during the term of four years, and, together with the Vice-President chosen for the same term, be elected as follows : —

Each State shall appoint, in such manner as the legislature thereof may direct, a number of electors, equal to the whole number of senators and representatives to which the State may be entitled in the Congress ; but no senator or representatives, or persons holding an office of trust or profit under the United States, shall be appointed an elector.

The Congress may determine the time of choosing the electors, and the day on which they shall give their votes ; which day shall be the same throughout the United States.

No person, except a natural-born citizen, or a citizen of the United States at the time of the adoption of this Constitution, shall be eligible to the office of President ; neither shall any person be eligible to that office who shall not have attained to the age of thirty-five years, and been fourteen years a resident within the United States.

In case of the removal of the President from office, or of his death, resignation, or inability to discharge the powers and duties of the said office, the same shall devolve on the Vice-President, and the Congress may by law provide for the case of removal, death, resignation, or inability, both of the President and Vice-President, declaring what officer shall then act as President, and such officer shall act accordingly, until the disability be removed, or a President shall be elected.

The President shall, at stated times, receive for his services a compensation, which shall neither be increased nor diminished during the period for which he shall have been elected, and he shall not receive within that period any other emolument from the United States, or any of them.

Before he enters on the execution of his office, he shall take the following oath or affirmation : —

"I do solemnly swear (or affirm) that I will faithfully execute the office of President of the United States, and will, to the best of my ability, preserve, protect, and defend the Constitution of the United States."

SEC. 2. The President shall be Commander-in-Chief of the army and navy of the United States, and of the militia of the several States, when called into the actual service of the United States ; he may require the opinion, in writing, of the principal officer in each of the executive departments, upon any subject relating to the duties of their respective offices, and he shall have power to grant reprieves and pardon for offenses against the United States, except in cases of impeachment.

He shall have power, by and with the advice and consent of the Senate, to make treaties, provided two thirds of the senators present concur ; and he shall nominate, and by and with the advice and consent of the Senate, shall appoint, ambassadors, other public ministers and consuls, judges of the Supreme Court, and all other officers of the United States whose appointments are not herein otherwise provided for, and which shall be established by law ; but the Congress may by law vest the appointment of such inferior officers as they think proper in the President alone, in the courts of law, or in the heads of departments.

The President shall have power to fill up all vacancies that may happen during the recess of the Senate, by granting commissions, which shall expire at the end of their next session.

SEC. 3. He shall from time to time give to the Congress information of the state of the Union, and recommend to their consideration such measures as he shall judge necessary and expedient; he may, on extraordinary occasions, convene both houses, or either of them, and in case of disagreement between them, with respect to the time of adjournment, he may adjourn them to such time as he shall think proper; he shall receive ambassadors and other public ministers; he shall take care that the laws be faithfully executed, and shall commission all the officers of the United States.

SEC. 4. The President, Vice-President, and all civil officers of the United States, shall be removed from office on impeachment for, and conviction of, treason, bribery, or other high crimes and misdemeanors.

ARTICLE III.

SECTION 1. The judicial power of the United States shall be vested in one Supreme Court, and in such inferior courts as the Congress may from time to time ordain and establish. The judges, both of the supreme and inferior courts, shall hold their offices during good behavior, and shall, at stated times, receive for their services a compensation which shall not be diminished during their continuance in office.

SEC. 2. The judicial power shall extend to all cases, in law and equity, arising under this Constitution, the laws of the United States, and treaties made, or which shall be made, under their authority; to all cases affecting ambassadors, other public ministers, and consuls; to all cases of admiralty and maritime jurisdiction; to controversies to which the United States shall be a party; to controversies between two or more States; between a State and citizens of another State; between citizens of different States; between citizens of the same State claiming lands under grants of different States, and between a State, or the citizens thereof, and foreign States, citizens, or subjects.

In all cases affecting ambassadors, other public ministers, and consuls, and those in which a State shall be party, the Supreme Court shall have original jurisdiction. In all the other cases before mentioned, the Supreme Court shall have appellate jurisdiction, both as to law and fact, with such exceptions and under such regulations as the Congress shall make.

The trial of all crimes, except in cases of impeachment, shall be by jury; and such trial shall be held in the State where the said crime shall have been committed; but when not committed within any State, the trial shall be at such place or places as the Congress may by law have directed.

SEC. 3. Treason against the United States shall consist only in levying war against them, or in adhering to their enemies, giving them aid and comfort. No person shall be convicted of treason unless on the testimony of two witnesses to the same overt act, or on confession in open court.

The Congress shall have power to declare the punishment of treason, but no attainder of treason shall work corruption of blood, or forfeiture except during the life of the person attainted.

ARTICLE IV.

SECTION 1. Full faith and credit shall be given in each State to the public acts, records, and judicial proceedings of every other State. And the Congress may by general laws prescribe the manner in which such acts, records, and proceedings shall be proved, and the effect thereof.

SEC. 2. The citizens of each State shall be entitled to all privileges and immunities of citizens in the several States.

A person charged in any State with treason, felony, or other crime, who shall flee from justice, and be found in another State, shall on demand of the executive authority of the State from which he fled, be delivered up, to be removed to the State having jurisdiction of the crime.

No person held to service or labor in one State, under the laws thereof, escaping into another, shall, in consequence of any law or regulation therein, be discharged from such service or labor, but shall be delivered up on claim of the party to whom such service or labor may be due.

SEC. 3. New States may be admitted by the Congress into this Union ; but no new State shall be formed or erected within the jurisdiction of any other State ; nor any State be formed by the junction of two or more States, or parts of States, without the consent of the legislatures of the States concerned, as well as of the Congress.

The Congress shall have power to dispose of and make all needful rules and regulations respecting the territory or other property belonging to the United States, and nothing in this Constitution shall be so construed as to prejudice any claims of the United States, or of any particular State.

SEC. 4. The United States shall guarantee to every State in this Union a republican form of government, and shall protect each of them against invasion, and, on application of the legislature or of the executive (when the legislature cannot be convened), against domestic violence.

ARTICLE V.

The Congress, whenever two thirds of both houses shall deem it necessary, shall propose amendments to this Constitution, or, on the application of the legislatures of two thirds of the several States, shall call a convention for proposing amendments, which, in either case, shall be valid, to all intents and purposes, as part of this Constitution, when ratified by the legislatures of three fourths of the several States, or by conventions in three fourths thereof, as the one or the other mode of ratification may be proposed by the Congress ; provided, that no amendment which may be made prior to the year one thousand eight hundred and eight shall in any manner affect the first and fourth clauses in the ninth section of the first Article, and that no State, without its consent, shall be deprived of its equal suffrage in the Senate.

Article VI.

All debts contracted and engagements entered into before the adoption of the Constitution, shall be as valid against the United States under this Constitution as under the Confederation.

This Constitution, and the laws of the United States which shall be made in pursuance thereof, and all treaties made, or which shall be made, under the authority of the United States, shall be the supreme law of the land ; and the judges in every State shall be bound thereby, anything in the Constitution or laws of any State to the contrary notwithstanding.

The senators and representatives before mentioned, and the members of the several State legislatures, and all executive and judicial officers, both of the United States and of the several States, shall be bound by oath or affirmation to support this Constitution ; but no religious test shall ever be required as a qualification to any office or public trust under the United States.

Article VII.

The ratification of the conventions of nine States shall be sufficient for the establishment of this Constitution between the States so ratifying the same.

AMENDMENTS TO THE CONSTITUTION.

Article I.

Congress shall make no law respecting an establishment of religion, or prohibiting the free exercise thereof ; or abridging the freedom of speech, or of the press ; or the right of the people peaceably to assemble, and to petition the Government for a redress of grievances.

Article II.

A well-regulated militia being necessary to the security of a free State, the right of the people to keep and bear arms shall not be infringed.

Article III.

No soldier shall, in time of peace, be quartered in any house without the consent of the owner, nor in time of war, but in a manner to be prescribed by law.

Article IV.

The right of the people to be secure in their persons, houses, papers, and effects, against unreasonable searches and seizures, shall not be violated ; and no warrants shall issue but upon probable cause, supported by oath or affirmation, and particularly describing the place to be searched, and the persons or things to be seized.

Article V.

No person shall be held to answer for a capital or otherwise infamous crime, unless on a presentment or indictment of a Grand Jury, except in cases arising in the land or naval forces, or in the militia, when in actual service, in time of war and public danger ; nor shall any person be subject for the same offense to be twice put in jeopardy of life or limb, nor shall be compelled in any criminal case to be a witness against himself ; nor to be deprived of life, liberty, or property, without due process of law ; nor shall private property be taken for public use without just compensation.

ARTICLE VI.

In all criminal prosecutions, the accused shall enjoy the right to a speedy and public trial, by an impartial jury of the State and district wherein the crime shall have been committed, which district shall have been previously ascertained by law, and to be informed of the nature and cause of the accusation ; to be confronted with the witnesses against him ; to have compulsory process for obtaining witnesses in his favor, and to have the assistance of counsel for his defense.

ARTICLE VII.

In suits at common law, where the value in controversy shall exceed twenty dollars, the right of trial by jury shall be preserved, and no fact tried by a jury shall be otherwise re-examined in any court of the United States than according to the rules of the common law.

ARTICLE VIII.

Excessive bail shall not be required, nor excessive fines be imposed, nor cruel and unusual punishments inflicted.

ARTICLE IX.

The enumeration in the Constitution of certain rights shall not be construed to deny or disparage others retained by the people.

ARTICLE X.

The powers not delegated to the United States by the Constitution, nor prohibited by it to the States, are reserved to the States respectively, or to the people.

ARTICLE XI.

The judicial power of the United States shall not be construed to extend to any suit in law or equity, commenced or prosecuted against one of the United States by citizens of another State, or by citizens or subjects of any foreign State.

ARTICLE XII.

The electors shall meet in their respective States, and vote by ballot for President and Vice-President, one of whom, at least, shall not be an inhabitant of the same State with themselves. They shall name in their ballots the person voted for as President, and in distinct ballots the person voted for as Vice-President ; and they shall make distinct lists of all persons voted for as President, and of all persons voted for as Vice-President, and of the number of votes for each, which lists they shall sign and certify, and transmit, sealed, to the seat of the Government of the United States, directed to the president of the Senate. The president of the Senate shall, in the presence of the Senate and House of Representatives, open all the certificates, and the votes shall then be counted : the person having the greatest number of votes for President shall be the President, if such number be a majority of the whole number of electors appointed ; and if no person have such majority, then from the persons having the highest numbers, not exceeding three, on the list of those voted for as President, the House of Representatives shall choose immediately, by ballot, the President. But in choosing the President, the votes shall be taken by States, the representation from each State having one vote ; a quorum for this purpose shall consist of a member or members from two thirds of the States, and a majority of all the States shall be necessary to a choice. And if the House of Representatives shall not choose a President, whenever the right of choice shall devolve upon them, before the fourth day of March next following, then the Vice-President shall act as President, as in the case of the death or other Constitutional disability of the President. The person having the greatest number of votes as Vice-President shall be the Vice-President, if such number be a majority of the whole number of electors appointed ; and if no person have a majority, then from the two highest numbers on the list, the Senate shall choose the Vice-President ; a quorum for the purpose shall consist of two thirds of the whole number of senators, and a majority of the whole number shall be necessary to a choice. But no person Constitutionally ineligible to the office of President shall be eligible to that of Vice-President of the United States.

ARTICLE XIII.

SECTION 1. Neither slavery nor involuntary servitude, except as a punishment for crime, whereof the party shall have been duly convicted, shall exist within the United States, or any place subject to their jurisdiction.

SEC. 2. Congress shall have power to enforce this article by appropriate legislation.

ARTICLE XIV.

SECTION 1. All persons born or naturalized in the United States, and subject to the jurisdiction thereof, are citizens of the United States, and of the State in which they reside. No State shall make or enforce any law which shall abridge the privileges or immunities of citizens of the United States ; nor shall any State deprive any person of life, liberty, or property without due process of law, nor deny to any person within its jurisdiction the equal protection of the laws.

SEC. 2. Representatives shall be apportioned among the several States according to their respective numbers, counting the whole number of persons in each State, excluding Indians not taxed. But when the right to vote at any election for the choice of electors for President and Vice-President of the United States, representatives in Congress, the executive and judicial officers of a State, or the members of the legislature **thereof, is** denied to any of the male inhabitants of such State being twenty-one **years** of age, and citizens of the **United States, or in any way** abridged, except **for** participation in rebellion or other crime, **the basis of** representation therein **shall** be reduced in **the propor-tion which the num**ber of such male citizens shall bear to the whole **number of** male citizens twenty-one years of age in such State.

SEC. 3. No person shall be a senator or representative in Congress, or elector of President and Vice-President, or hold any office, civil or military, un-der the United States, or under any State, who, having previously taken an oath as a member of Congress, or as an officer of the United States, or as a member of any State legislature, or as an executive or judicial officer of any State, to support the Constitution of the United States, shall have engaged in insurrection or rebellion against the same, or given aid or comfort to the ene-mies thereof. But Congress may, by a vote of two thirds of each house, re-move such disability.

SEC. 4. The validity of the public **debt of** the United States authorized by **law,** including debts incurred by payment of pensions and bounties for services **in suppressing** insurrection **or** rebellion, shall not be questioned. But neither **the United States nor any** State shall assume or pay **any** debt or obliga-**tion incurred in aid of insurrection or** rebellion against the United States, **or any claim for the loss or emancipation of** any slave ; but all such debts, obliga-**tions, and claims shall be held illegal and void.**

SEC. 5. The Congress shall have power to enforce, by appropriate legisla-tion, the provisions of this article.

ARTICLE XV.

SECTION 1. The right of the citizens of the United States to vote shall not be denied or abridged by the United States, or by any State, on account of race, color, or previous condition of servitude.

SEC. 2. The Congress shall have power to enforce this article by appropriate legislation.